All Things Testify of Him

All Things Testify of Him

INSPIRATIONAL
PAINTINGS BY
LATTER-DAY
SAINT ARTISTS

BOOKCRAFT
Salt Lake City, Utah

Library of Congress Catalog Card Number: 98-73232

ISBN 1-57008-532-3

Second Printing, 1999

Printed in the United States of America

Color Separations by WHN, Salt Lake City, Utah
Printed at Publishers Press

Contents

Baptism, by Julie Ann Buhler,
12" x 12", intaglio, 1997

∽

∽

Introduction

"*A*ll great art is the expression of man's delight in God's work, not his own," said John Ruskin, the great nineteenth-century English art critic. In 2 Nephi 11:4, Nephi declares, "Behold my soul delighteth in proving unto my people the truth of the coming of Christ; for, for this end hath the law of Moses been given; and all things which have been given of God from the beginning of the world, unto man, are the typifying of him."

All things testify of Jesus Christ, the Savior of the world. And some of the finest examples of this principle can be found in the paintings of Latter-day Saint artists who seek to bear witness of the Savior through their work.

All Things Testify of Him brings together the work of Greg Olsen, Al Rounds, Del Parson, Judith Mehr, Liz Lemmon Swindle, Robert T. Barrett, Frank Magleby, and many other gifted painters. The artists have selected paintings that serve as expressions of their own faith and personal testimony and, in addition, have provided accompanying texts that explain the inspiration behind each painting included in this work. Touching testimonies of the Savior are woven through the simplicity of these artists' words and the power of their art.

Commenting on his paintings, James Christensen writes: "When the painter and the viewer are in sync, the work can communicate on a nonverbal, aesthetic, even a spiritual level. . . . People ask me if I paint many religious paintings, and I respond that all my work is part of my testimony and belief system."

Indeed, each artist bears record of Him in a unique and moving way through the colors, figures, and spirit incorporated into his or her paintings. These artists are certainly considered outstanding in their field, but more than that, they are what Elder M. Russell Ballard calls spiritually successful. "Spiritually successful artists," he says, "have the unique opportunity to present their feelings, opinions, ideas, and perspectives of eternity in visual and sound symbols that are universally understood. Great art touches the soul in unique and uncommon ways. Divinely inspired art speaks in the language of eternity, teaching things to the heart that the eyes and the ears can never understand." ("Filling the World with Goodness and Truth," *Ensign*, July 1996, p. 10.)

The art presented in *All Things Testify of Him* speaks of eternity. It bears witness of the Savior of the world and encourages the viewer to look within and recognize the beauty of every thing on this earth that testifies of Jesus Christ.

"And behold, all things have their likeness, and all things are created and made to bear record of me, both things which are temporal, and things which are spiritual; things which are in the heavens above, and things which are on the earth, and things which are in the earth, and things which are under the earth, both above and beneath: all things bear record of me" (Moses 6:63). ∾

Antecedent, by Jennifer Hillam Barton,
19-1/2" x 25-1/2", pastel on paper, 1997

The Well of Life, by Robert T. Barrett, 34" x 24", oil on board, 1996

THE WELL OF LIFE

I have always loved the story of Jesus and the Samaritan woman (see John 4). As Jesus left Judea for Galilee, he traveled through Samaria and rested at Jacob's well. For some time there existed strong antagonism between the Jews and the Samaritans. Not only did Jesus bring down traditional barriers between the cultures through events like this one but he also sought to elevate the position of both women and children numerous times.

The narrative begins with Jesus sitting near the well. In my mind I envision the well as an oasis in the desert—a cool and shaded place offering a haven for the traveler. As the woman arrives and the dialogue evolves into a teaching opportunity, I have chosen to show Christ standing and taking an active role in the conversation. It doesn't take long for the woman to perceive that he is a prophet by the things he says and knows about her. He speaks to her metaphorically of living water that he has to give. I wanted to use the cool colors of blue and green, contrasted with the warmer background, to symbolize the story in visual terms. The olive tree arches over both figures, offering protection and drawing them together. The coolness of the foreground elements equates, in various ways, with the refreshing nature of the message Jesus has to impart. ∾

Robert T. Barrett

SOLOMON DEDICATES THE TEMPLE

*I*n Jerusalem, Solomon built a beautiful temple to house the ark of the covenant. It proved to be his crowning achievement and was dedicated by him in an impressive ceremony about 952 B. C. "And Solomon stood before the altar of the Lord in the presence of all the congregation of Israel, and spread forth his hands toward heaven" (1 Kings 8:22). At the conclusion of the prayer, Solomon and the people of Israel offered sacrifices to the Lord. And when Solomon was alone, the Lord appeared to him a second time (see 1 Kings 9).

In addition to its religious significance, the completion of the temple signified the permanence of Jerusalem as God's worldly capital and of the House of David as Israel's ruling family. ∾

*Solomon Dedicates the Temple
by Robert T. Barrett,
22" x 28",
oil on canvas,
1989*

Ruth Gleaning

After Ruth returned to Bethlehem with her mother-in-law, Naomi, they found that the time of famine in Judah was past. A large supply of grain waited to be gathered, and the harvesting was difficult work, demanding long hours. Young men moved through the fields, first grasping handfuls of grain and cutting through the stalks with sickles. As the men worked rapidly, a number of stalks fell to the ground. Poor people, following the reapers, were permitted to glean, or gather, the random stalks.

Because Naomi was too old to work in the fields, Ruth offered to work for both of them. Eventually she won the favor of Boaz, married him, and had a son who became the grandfather of King David. Through her lineage would later be born the Savior, Jesus Christ. (See Ruth 2–4.)

My wife, Vicki, and I had the opportunity to stand in Shepherds' Field near Bethlehem and recount the events of Ruth's life, her devotion and dedication, and her subsequent success. ॐ

*Ruth Gleaning,
by Robert T. Barrett,
22" x 28",
oil on canvas,
1992*

Hurrah, Hurrah, Hurrah for Israel

On September 18, 1839, despite the fact that they were both sick with malaria, Brigham Young and Heber C. Kimball departed on their mission to England. They mounted a wagon owned by neighbor Charles Hubbard and driven by his teenage son. Heber's wife, Vilate, was lying sick in bed with two of his children, and little Heber Parley was the only one well enough to carry water to the sick. Mary Ann Young, who had a new baby, had come from Montrose to help nurse Brigham before the departure.

From Heber C. Kimball's diary we read: "With some difficulty we got into the wagon and started down the hill about ten rods. It seemed to me as though my very inmost parts would melt within me at the thought of leaving my family in such a condition, as it were almost in the arms of death. I felt as though I could scarcely endure it. I said to the teamster 'hold up!' then turning to Brother Brigham, I added, 'This is pretty tough, but let's rise, and give them a cheer.' We arose, and swinging our hats three times over our heads, we cried, 'Hurrah, hurrah, hurrah for Israel!'

"My wife, hearing the noise, arose from her bed and came to the door to see what was up. She had a smile on her face. She and Sister Young cried out to us, 'Good bye; God bless you!' We returned the compliment and were pleased to see that they were so cheerful. We then told the driver to go ahead." (As quoted in Stanley B. Kimball, "Heber C. Kimball and Family, The Nauvoo Years," *BYU Studies* [Provo: Brigham Young University Press, Summer 1975], p. 450.)

In the spring of 1997 I had the opportunity to walk down the same Nauvoo road traveled by Brigham and Heber. As I looked back toward the Heber C. Kimball home, which now stands on the site where the cabin was, I imagined what it must have been like for the two intrepid missionaries to leave their families in such a condition. I decided to illustrate the story through their eyes so the viewer looks back at the scene they could have encountered. ॐ

Hurrah, Hurrah, Hurrah for Israel, by Robert T. Barrett, 72" x 48", oil on canvas, 1997

FLIGHT INTO EGYPT

Shortly after Jesus' birth, King Herod, the ruler of Palestine, learned that wise men had followed a star from the East to Bethlehem, where they believed the Messiah had been born. Fearing that his throne might be in danger, Herod ordered all male children under the age of two to be killed.

Before Herod could destroy the infant Jesus, an angel appeared to Joseph in a dream and instructed him to "take the young child and his mother, and flee into Egypt" (Matthew 2:13). Joseph arose and took Mary and her infant son and departed by night into Egypt.

I have tried to show both the anxiety and determination in the figures of Joseph and Mary as they, through their faith, followed the admonition of the angel and traveled with but a few provisions into a strange land. ❧

Flight into Egypt,
by Robert T. Barrett,
24" x 36",
oil on canvas,
1985

THE PIONEER

*A*lthough the pioneers who crossed the plains encountered physical exhaustion, intense heat, bitter cold, and a variety of other hardships, there was another side to the story as well. The level prairie, covered with lush grass and dotted with larkspur, verbena, lupine, and geranium was a glorious sight to behold. Though there was suffering, deprivation, and even death, the triumph over difficulties more than compensated for their efforts and made the overland passage a thing never to be forgotten.

I had the opportunity to go to graduate school at the University of Iowa in Iowa City, Iowa. My wife and I lived not far from the location of the handcart sites and had the experience of driving across the plains several times between there and Salt Lake City. We traveled in all kinds of weather conditions and saw many vistas with expansive skies and memorable sunsets.

This painting was created for the Fourth International Juried Art Competition held at the Museum of Church History and Art. It received an award of excellence in the show, and the museum subsequently purchased it. ❧

The Pioneer, by Robert T. Barrett, 22" x 28", oil on canvas, 1997

CHRIST'S BAPTISM

Shortly after John the Baptist began his public ministry, news reached Nazareth that a prophet had appeared in the wilderness preaching the repentance of sins and proclaiming that the long-awaited king was at hand. Jesus came from Galilee to Jordan, where he was baptized by John "to fulfill all righteousness" and set an example for "the children of men" to follow (2 Nephi 31:5–7).

Luke tells us: "when all the people were baptized, it came to pass, that Jesus also being baptized" (Luke 3:21). This indicates that there were other people present. Luke also explains that "the Holy Ghost descended in a bodily shape like a dove upon him, and a voice came from heaven, which said, Thou art my beloved Son; in thee I am well pleased" (Luke 3:22). ❧

Christ's Baptism, by Robert T. Barrett,
18" x 24", oil on board, 1996

BRING FORTH THE RECORD

*A*fter his death and resurrection, Jesus Christ appeared to the Nephites who were assembled at the temple in the land Bountiful. He called twelve disciples, taught the Nephites how to pray, instituted the sacrament, and healed the sick. He commanded the people to search the words of the prophets and write the words he spoke unto them. He then asked that the record kept be brought forth and instructed the Nephites to add to the record the prophesies of Samuel the Lamanite. He then expounded to them all the scriptures that they had written and instructed them to teach those things. (See 3 Nephi 11–36.)

The twelve disciples surrounding the Savior in my painting are representative of diversity in culture and age. Many sacred truths were imparted only to them and not to the multitudes. The records portrayed in the painting represent records kept in different forms and in different medias. Christ is at the center and appears as the lightest light against the darkest dark. ❧

Bring Forth the Record, by Robert T. Barrett, 28" x 22", oil on board, 1985

ABOUT THE ARTIST

*R*obert T. Barrett, an accomplished painter, muralist, and illustrator, is a professor of illustration at Brigham Young University. His work has been exhibited in art shows across the country and in Germany.

Robert received a bachelor of fine arts degree in painting from the University of Utah and master of arts and master of fine arts degrees in painting from the University of Iowa. He completed a year of post-graduate work in Germany at the Hochshule der Künste in Berlin.

His clientele includes Viking USA, Random House, Fawcett Books, Harper Collins, Bantam, Double Day Dell Publications, Thomas Nelson, Ideals Publishing, and *McCalls* magazine. For a number of years his work has appeared in LDS Church publications, including the *Ensign, New Era,* and *The Friend. The Work and the Glory* series, published by Bookcraft, features many of Robert's illustrations on the early history of the LDS Church.

His *Portraits of the Prophets* series is on permanent display in the Harman Building at BYU, and various other paintings hang in a number of LDS temples and visitors centers throughout the world. ❧

Wulf Erich Barsch

*T*hese paintings all relate to the involvement of the gospel with cosmology, astronomy, and, specifically, the relation of Ursa Major and Orion to our understanding of the endowment.

I've never gotten over the idea that somehow Egypt is our schoolmaster. Joseph Smith knew that the Egyptians had real archaic wisdom. The ancient order, as he called it, and our temples are full of references to eternal life and its connected cosmology. While everyone else throughout the ages threw up their hands in hopelessness at the terrible questions surrounding the cosmos, the ancient Egyptians never gave up asking and praying for answers. ❧

Toward the Holy Mountain, by Wulf Erich Barsch,
52" x 72", oil on canvas, 1992

Untitled, by Wulf Erich Barsch, 72" x 52", oil on canvas, 1991

Untitled, by Wulf Erich Barsch, 60" x 84", oil on canvas, 1990

Untitled, by Wulf Erich Barsch,
42" x 72", oil on canvas, 1998

12

ABOUT THE ARTIST

*W*ulf Erich Barsch was born August 27, 1943, in Reudnitz, Bohemia. He studied printmaking and painting at Werkkunstschule, Hannover, Germany; and Staatliche Hochschule fur Bildende Künste in Hamburg, Germany. He received a master's degree in printmaking from Brigham Young University in 1971 and a master of fine arts degree in painting from BYU in 1972.

Wulf is a professor in the Department of Art at BYU. He and his wife, Sandra Porter Barsch, are the parents of five children. ❧

Untitled, by Wulf Erich Barsch, 60" x 78",
oil on marble ground on panel, 1997

THE GIFT

*T*his painting is about the gift of life. A woman standing in front of a door with a beckoning hand is symbolic of the fact that we are all born into mortality through the body of a woman. A woman is a portal for life. Our first mother, Eve, was the one who got the "apple" rolling in the Garden of Eden when she chose to partake of the fruit of the tree of knowledge of good and evil.

The cross motif in the transom above the door represents our physical death and the Atonement. The lilies represent the Resurrection. These are the great gifts of life that Jesus Christ gave so freely to us all. The door also represents our passage through the portals of birth, death, and rebirth, both physically and spiritually. ❧

The Gift, by Lee Udall Bennion,
30" x 56", oil on canvas, 1991

THE GUARDIANS

*T*his painting comes from many late evening and early morning walks in my town of Spring City, Utah. I never tire of looking at the carefully crafted yet humble pioneer dwellings that are still here in great numbers or the many out buildings that dot the old quarter block lots. When my older girls were young they asked me about some of the old poplar trees that, although dead, were still standing like guardians near some of the homesteads. I told them that they were "pioneer trees," planted by the first settlers because they grew fast and would soon supply shade for the home and yard.

I think of these poplars, black locust, and other varieties of trees as representatives of our forefathers and mothers who gave so much of themselves as they settled here in the west. These old trees and hand-hewn homes speak to me of their love, struggles, and sacrifices. I feel that they symbolically are guardians of the faith planted and built upon by the pioneers. ∾

ABOUT THE ARTIST

*L*ee Udall Bennion was born in Merced, California, in 1956 to Addison and Ada Webster Udall. She grew up in Merced and came to Utah in 1974 to begin studies at BYU. In 1976 she married fellow art student Joseph Bennion. Joseph is a potter.

Lee and Joe moved to Spring City, Utah, shortly after their marriage and have spent the last twenty-two years raising a family of three daughters, growing numerous gardens, and painting and potting. They are members of the Spring City Second Ward.

Lee has received two annual artist's grants from the Utah Arts Council as well as a visual arts fellowship and purchase award from the "Utah '88" painting and sculpture exhibition.

Lee's work is on display throughout Utah and Arizona. ∾

The Guardians, by Lee Udall Bennion,
30" x 56", oil on linen, 1991

Bruce Brainard

JOURNEY

*A*s an artist, I use the landscape as a metaphor for fallen man and his quest for light, peace, and meaning. My paintings are an attempt to describe the spiritual odyssey of the soul of man from a lone and dreary world, cut off from the presence of God, back to His sphere, a state of light and peace. I utilize the universal symbols of nature to portray the journey.

In *Journey* the viewer is in a river, the river of life, confronted by a row of deciduous trees that separate them from an inviting light. The viewer must pass through the trees, symbolic of death—death of the natural man—to attain the light. ∾

Journey, by Bruce Brainard, 72" x 52", oil, 1990

ABOUT THE ARTIST

*B*ruce Brainard has worked as a professional artist since 1989. He is currently working with a number of galleries throughout the United States, including Gremillion and Company Fine Arts in Houston, Texas; Macon & Company Fine Art in Atlanta, Georgia; Lisa Kurt's gallery in Memphis, Tennessee; and Wyndy Morehead Gallery in New Orleans, Louisiana.

His love of landscapes first began with his childhood in a small farming community nestled under the Tetons in the upper Snake River Valley of southeastern Idaho. This love was further intensified while, as a young man, he worked in the fields, observing the land and pondering the meaning of life.

He began his professional studies in 1980 at Brigham Young University, majoring in fine art. From 1981 to 1983 he served an LDS mission to Coventry, England. He returned to BYU and finished his bachelor's degree with an emphasis in oil painting in 1988.

It was at BYU, while working with Wulf Barsh, that he was first introduced to the spiritual significance of art. Wulf also opened his eyes to the spiritual promptings he had felt as a young man enwrapped in the landscape.

After a brief period developing his craft outside the structure of the university he returned to BYU and obtained a master of fine arts degree in 1992.

Since that time he has been working as a professional artist with a home and studio in Pleasant Grove, Utah. His loves include his wife, Lori, good friends, thought-provoking discussions, reading, exercise, golf, and skiing. ∾

James C. Christensen

SOMETIMES THE SPIRIT TOUCHES US THROUGH OUR WEAKNESSES

*T*he hunchback is my symbol for every man—imperfect, with a visible burden to bear. It might be common knowledge to Latter-day Saints that God gives us weaknesses to help us become strong, but that idea is not necessarily universal. While this appears to be a fantasy painting, it addresses an important truth about our lives here on earth. And I have watched people respond very positively to the message of this piece as they realize how they have grown through adversity. ❧

Sometimes the Spirit Touches Us Through Our Weaknesses, by James C. Christensen, 12" x 16", oil, 1992

GETHSEMANE

*T*his painting comes from Luke 22:43. "And there appeared an angel unto him from heaven, strengthening him." I was trying to understand the Atonement when I painted this piece, and I was very taken by this verse. One way that we are strengthened is through priesthood blessings. Perhaps the angel came to give the Savior a blessing to help him endure the trial in the garden. Elder Bruce R. McConkie speculated that the angel was Michael, even Adam, the first man. There is a beautiful symmetry to this idea. Two gardens, two individuals; one to allow man to exist and progress, the other to free man from death and sin. In the first garden Jehovah teaches Adam, in the second garden Michael blesses Christ. ❧

Gethsemane, by James C. Christensen,
acrylic, 1984

THE WIDOW'S MITE

*T*he widow in this painting from the New Testament is young and beautiful. Michelangelo was criticized for making Mary look as young as her son in his statue of the *Pietà*. He replied that her virtue made her beautiful. I thought about that when I painted this painting. ❧

The Widow's Mite, by James C. Christensen,
30" x 24", oil, 1986

The Responsible Woman,
by James C. Christensen,
24" x 18", acrylic, 1992

THE RESPONSIBLE WOMAN

*T*his painting pays homage to women and the many facets of their lives.
While she may just barely stay above the tops of the trees, she is constantly looking ahead and holds aloft the light that guides her family. ᐧᐧ

ALLEGORY AT ALGARVE

*T*his is an early painting conceived while on a train with students in Europe. It was my first trip abroad and I was so excited about everything I saw. One afternoon we were traveling through the Alps, and I was drinking in the scenery while my students, three weeks on the road, never looked up from their card game to notice the magnificent mountains. I wonder how many of us get so involved with our petty activities in dark corners of our lives that we never really look up to see the beauty of eternity, or heaven, which is what the beach represents to me. ❧

Allegory at Algarve, by James C. Christensen, acrylic, 1981

SOLO

*T*his was part of a series of paintings on our interaction with each other. The man in the middle says, "I am alone." The two figures hurrying away state, "All is in the hands of God." It was years later that, as I looked at this painting in my living room, I saw the cruciform created by the words and realized that there was another whole layer of meaning I had not been aware of when I painted this piece. Many of my paintings have revealed themselves to me after a significant period of time. ∾

Solo, by James C. Christensen,
24" x 18", acrylic, 1988

Opus 96, by James C. Christensen,
23-1/2" x 18", oil, 1996

OPUS 96

*T*his is a kind of self-portrait. Every ten years I do a painting about myself and how I view death. This is the third work in the series. As I turned fifty a friend said, "At fifty you are not at the end of the tunnel, but you can *see* the end of the tunnel from here." ❧

Mary, by James C. Christensen, acrylic, 1985

MARY

*T*his was a study for a painting of the Annunciation. I wanted to portray Mary as a young woman pondering the most important message ever delivered to an individual on this earth. ❧

THE WINDOWS OF HEAVEN

*T*his portrait of Lorenzo Snow was painted at the time they were renovating the St. George Temple. I asked the Church photographer to take a picture of a window of the temple to put behind President Snow. It refers to the revelation on tithing. ❧

The Windows of Heaven, by James C. Christensen,
12" x 16", acrylic, 1978

ABOUT THE ARTIST

$\mathcal{J}$ames C. Christensen is a man of many talents and pursuits. In addition to his full-time work as an artist, he recently retired from Brigham Young University where he taught as a professor of art for twenty-one years. He has also been involved in printmaking, costume and scenery design, and film. His art has been the focus of fifteen one-man shows throughout North America and more than one hundred group shows, including the International Conference on the Fantastic in Houston, Texas; the First and Second Exhibition of the National Academy of Fantastic Art, Delaware Art Museum; and NASA's "Vision of Other Worlds" exhibit.

Of his work James says: "Painting is about communication. At its best, it communicates on a number of levels. The viewer is engaged by the image, the color, the design, the presence of the piece, and, with a little effort and time, identifies an emotional content, a message, a feeling about the work. When the painter and the viewer are in sync, the work can transcend all of this and communicate on a nonverbal, aesthetic, perhaps even a spiritual level. Not every work I create attempts to achieve all of this. I want my paintings to delight, amuse, enlighten, and challenge the viewer. I hope that I offer a slightly different point of view to a subject, providing a new insight for the viewer or a shared experience or perhaps a moment of enlightenment. People ask me if I paint many religious paintings, and I respond that all my work is part of my testimony and my belief system. Some are simply more obvious than others."

James has completed two books, *Journey of the Imagination, The Art of James C. Christensen,* and *The Voyage of the Basset,* a fantasy adventure illustrated with ninety-six new paintings. He currently lives with his family in Orem, Utah. ❧

QUILT

*I*n tribute to the sacrifice of our pioneer forefathers, *Quilt* focuses on the most important symbols of the early days of the Church. Featured most prominently in the quilt are four of the early temples of this dispensation, each one constructed at great sacrifice in times of scarcity.

Each corner of the image pays homage to the great events associated with the restoration of the gospel. The bottom left corner is a depiction of the First Vision; the right bottom corner portrays the restoration of the Aaronic Priesthood; the top right corner recalls the exodus from Winter Quarters; and the top left corner celebrates the Saints' arrival to the Salt Lake Valley.

The homes that adorn the perimeter of the image each belong to Joseph Smith or Brigham Young. Starting at the bottom left corner and proceeding clockwise, the homes are: Joseph Smith's Palmyra home, Joseph Smith's Kirtland home, Brigham Young's Nauvoo home, Joseph Smith's Mansion House in Nauvoo, the Seventies Hall in Nauvoo, the St. George winter home of Brigham Young, Brigham Young's farmhouse in Salt Lake City, and the Lion House. ∾

ABOUT THE ARTIST

*E*ric Dowdle was born and raised in the heart of the western United States—Wyoming, Idaho, Utah, and Texas. For a short period of time Eric lived with his family in Boston, Massachusetts. During this time he developed a fascination with folk art. Eric is from a family of twelve children, ten boys and two girls. His parents taught basic principles that he feels show up in his art. Old fashioned values of hard work and devotion to God and country, as well as a peaceful spirit seemed to permeate every activity of his youth. Eric has an indomitable will, a powerful work ethic, and a natural, unbiased artistic eye for form and color. Blending these elements he creates art that seems to pop from the page in vivid colors, uncharacteristic of the watercolors he uses.

Eric opened his first gallery in the Cottonwood Mall in Salt Lake City. His work has been displayed in historical pageants across the country, and his work with the Amish is internationally recognized. Of the many rewards he has received for his Americana-style paintings, none is more flattering to him than the award he received in 1992 for his painting *Quilt* at the 1997 LDS Church art competition.

Eric has two children that seem to find their way into many of his pieces. He makes his home in Utah and has no intentions of settling elsewhere. ∾

Quilt, by Eric Dowdle, 26" x 32", watercolor, 1997

OLSEN PARK

*T*f you have ever been to Logan in the winter and witnessed the temple lit up in the frosty air, you know that it's a sight indeed! This turn-of-the-century piece depicts the fellowship and harmony that is associated with a religious small town. For the past one hundred years this park has been flooded to create a scene of winter wonderland.

Many first dates and proposals have been performed here with the perfect backdrop to accentuate the evening. Logan has a charm that I've tried to capture in the sense that the people thrive on what matters most in their lives: family, friends, and God. ❧

Olsen Park, by Eric Dowdle, 27" x 24", watercolor, 1997

St. George, Utah, by Eric Dowdle,
32" x 26", watercolor, 1996

ST. GEORGE, UTAH

St. George is one of those towns in Utah that as an artist you have to paint. The red cliffs surrounding the awesome brightness of the temple, the red brick buildings, and the genuine attitude of the people make perfect models.

As I did research at the historical society and met longtime residents of St. George, I discovered many stories to tell. What a rich piece of Latter-day Saint heritage! Gleaning all this information and trying to put it into one painting was a very enjoyable task. All of the buildings, for example, are on the historic register. I've included several businesses from the turn of the century, with the temple being the focal point. Twenty-four American flags represent the patriotism of Utah's Dixie. I tried to incorporate much detail and history into this painting so that anyone who has ever been to St. George can walk up and identify something personal to them, whether it's religious or merely nostalgic. ☙

PRAYER & DEDICATION OF THE SALT LAKE VALLEY—ORSON PRATT

*T*his event occurred the morning of July 23, 1847, in a grove of cottonwood trees on City Creek at the place where the Salt Lake City-County Building now stands. ∾

Prayer & Dedication of the Salt Lake Valley—Orson Pratt,
by VaLoy Eaton, 54" x 36", oil, 1996

JACOB HAMBLIN—THREE STRAYS

*B*righam Young sent the great pioneer, Jacob Hamblin, as a missionary to the Indians in Southern Utah. He had a profound influence on the Indian people, and they respected and trusted him. He established his home in Santa Clara, Utah. ∾

Jacob Hamblin—Three Strays, by VaLoy Eaton,
54" x 36", oil, 1997

Joseph Smith and the Nauvoo Temple,
by VaLoy Eaton, oil on board, 1989

JOSEPH SMITH AND THE NAUVOO TEMPLE

*A*s the Prophet Joseph Smith rode away from Nauvoo toward Carthage, he "paused when they got to the Temple, and looked with admiration first on that, and then on the city, and remarked, 'This is the loveliest place and the best people under the heavens; little do they know the trials that await them.'" Later he said, "I am going like a lamb to the slaughter, but I am calm as a summer's morning. I have a conscience void of offense toward God and toward all men." (*History of the Church*, 6:554, 555.) ❧

FIRST PLOWING

*O*n July 23, 1847, the day before Brigham Young arrived in the valley, the first furrows were turned at what is now Main Street and 100 South. Several plows were broken because the soil was very dry. That afternoon a dam was built across City Creek, and the ground was flooded. After that, the plowing was much easier. ∾

First Plowing,
by VaLoy Eaton,
54" x 36",
oil, 1997

ABOUT THE ARTIST

*V*aLoy Eaton paints quiet subjects with a universal message—a message of truth, life, and light. He believes that some of the most profound subjects are found in everyday occurrences and, if captured in paint, can forever remind us of special moments in time.

VaLoy was born and raised in Vernal, Utah, a farming and ranching community in eastern Utah at the foot of the Uintah Mountains. A few years ago he moved back to his hometown after living elsewhere for more than thirty years. He left Vernal in 1956 to attend Brigham Young University on a basketball scholarship. After graduation he taught art and coached sports for ten years in the Salt Lake City area, then returned to BYU to receive his master's degree in painting and design in 1971. Since then he has been very popular in collections all over the United States. He has participated in most of the major western shows as well as other important exhibits across the country. He is a four-time medal winner at the National Academy of Western Art.

He was appointed by the governor of Utah to serve on the Utah Arts Council, representing the visual arts for the state. His portrait hangs in Abravanel Hall, home of the Utah Symphony, as an "Honor in the Arts" recipient.

VaLoy and his wife, Ellie, have one daughter and four sons. ∾

Derek Hegsted

JOURNEY'S END

*T*he storm you weathered,
faithfully stood.
I was beside you
all the way
whisp'ring, you could!

Well done my faithful servant,
for me, you defended.
You stayed your course
your journey has ended. ∾

Journey's End, by Derek Hegsted,
24" x 30", oil, 1994

FEAR OF HOPE

$\mathcal{F}$eeling the desperation for the loss of Christ's body, Mary lingered at the tomb. She drew close the piece of linen, her only link to Christ, the cloth that had enveloped the torn and abused body of her best friend, her Savior. She was moved to it as if it were the only thing to keep her alive, as if it had a comforting force. She could control the fierce pain no longer and wept for the incredible loss. Then a voice said to her, "Woman, why weepest thou?" Thinking in earthly logic and casting aside the feeling of a familiar voice, she said, "Sir, if thou have borne him hence, tell me where thou hast laid him, and I will take him away." With a tender voice he uttered but one word, "Mary." (John 20: 14–16.) Joy swelling within her, she turned to the light, fearing to hope when it seemed it could not be.

Because of a woman's nature, Christ chose Mary Magdalene as the first witness of the Resurrection. This painting is my tribute to women. ❧

Fear of Hope, by Derek Hegsted, 48" x 36", oil, 1991

CHRIST'S PRAYER IN BOUNTIFUL
(detail of the light bearer)

*T*his man represents the sacred moment in which faith is changed to pure knowledge. Words cannot express the joy that he is feeling. It is a freedom only to be expressed with tears of gratitude and joy. This man wants to experience the presence of Christ with every human sense possible: *sight*—to see the glorious being that loves us beyond our understanding; *scent*—to smell the sweet scent of righteousness that he has never experienced before; *touch*—to hold him as he holds us, to caress the gentle, strong feet that walked to water, to touch the beautifully sculptured hands that healed the sick, raised the dead, calmed the sea, and cleansed the leper. These wonderful, strong hands restored reverence to the temple and cast out evil for a soul to have peace. Then these gentle, loving hands opened one last time to welcome the nails of the only atoning sacrifice Father in Heaven would ever accept. With every fiber and sensation of his body and mind, he desires to grasp his Savior's cloak and bury his tear-stained face in the Savior's embrace. This he knows will bring long-sought healing to his soul. ∾

*Christ's Prayer in Bountiful, by Derek Hegsted,
33" x 44", oil, 1997*

ABOUT THE ARTIST

*D*erek Hegsted was born in Provo, Utah, and raised in Idaho Falls, Idaho. He served an LDS mission to Tallahassee, Florida, after which he attended Ricks College on an art scholarship. There he earned associate degrees in fine arts and illustration. After graduation, Derek won an international illustration contest in which he competed with illustrators from thirty countries. He was then signed by Bantam Books of New York and Bridge Publications of Hollywood.

In 1991 he set aside illustration to go into religious fine art. Derek is a classical realist who uses the verdaccio underpainting method, the same style used by Renaissance masters such as Rembrandt, Bouguereau, and da Vinci. As a result, a single painting can take as long as a year to complete. Derek retains his originals so that he may exhibit them in museums and church buildings where everyone may enjoy them.

Derek has painted six paintings thus far, many of which have been published in LDS Church publications and on book and music covers.

Derek and his wife, Jolynn, have three children and reside in Orem, Utah. ∾

"I Will Not Fail Thee," by Derek Hegsted, 30" x 24", oil, 1993

"I WILL NOT FAIL THEE"

*W*hen you return to his strong arms, you will recognize the wounds in the palms of his hands and you will cry to him, "Who has caused this pain?" He will reply, "These are the wounds I received in the house of my friends. Yet, they fulfilled our Father's plan and are of infinite worth to thee." As he sur-rounds you with his loving embrace, the Spirit sweetly reminds you of the time before your birth. He held you gently, whispering loving words of assurance:

"I will not forget thee, nor forsake thee. I will not fail thee . . ."

And then you were born. ☙

Forging Onward, Ever Onward, by Glen S. Hopkinson, 60" x 30", oil, 1994

Glen S. Hopkinson

Forging Onward, Ever Onward

*P*ressure to leave Nauvoo was immense, at times, with gun battles raging in streets overwhelmed by the enemies who wanted the Saints out. I depicted that desperate exodus with Brigham Young and some armed brethren watching over the ill-prepared and disorganized Saints as they fled into the winter cold. Louisa Barnes Pratt, wife of Addison Pratt, tells of her feelings:

"At length the time came that we must leave our beloved temple, our city, our homes. Almon Babbit called to see me. I asked him if he could divine the reason why those who had sent my husband to the ends of the earth [a mission to the Pacific Islands] did not call to inquire whether I could prepare myself for such a perilous journey. His reply was, 'Sister Pratt, they expect you to be smart enough to go yourself without help, and even to assist others.' The remark awakened in me a spirit of self-reliance. I replied, 'Well, I will show them what I can do.'" (Louisa Barnes Pratt, Autobiography, *Heart Throbs of the West,* in Milton V. Backman, Jr., and Keith W. Perkins, eds. *Writings of Early Latter-day Saints and Their Contemporaries, A Database Collection.* Provo, Utah: Brigham Young University Religious Studies Center, 1996.) ∾

About the Artist

*G*len S. Hopkinson has loved the tales of the past his entire life. Now, as he paints history, he is able to bring those stories to life for others to see. Born and reared in Wyoming, Glen Hopkinson began painting full time in 1971. His interest in art began at his father's knee, using cast-off brushes his father would give him, saying, "If you can paint with these brushes you'll be able to paint anything!" His father is the well-known western artist Harold I. Hopkinson.

Melding his interests in history and art has brought him great success. His ability to visually tell a good story is one of the most striking features of his art. That skill proved useful in doing the storyboards and production design for the pioneer movie "Legacy."

Glen's artwork is in permanent collections of the Montana and Wyoming Historical Society museums, the Buffalo Bill Historical Center Winchester Museum, the Franklin-Covey building in Salt Lake City, and many other public and private collections around the world.

Glen and his wife, Pamela, presently live in Mesa, Arizona, and spend their summers in Wyoming. They have five children and three grandchildren. He credits his wife as a great source of help and encouragement. "I couldn't have done it without her." ∾

THE END OF PARLEY STREET

A few years ago in Nauvoo, I walked to the end of Parley Street imagining the hustle and bustle of the Saints as they prepared to leave. At the water's edge I looked back and felt some poignancy as I visualized the City on a Hill.

Brigham Young recorded these details of their departure: "Three congressmen came [to Nauvoo] in the fall of 1845. . . . They were desirous that we should leave the United States. . . . Stephen A. Douglas, one of the three, had been acquainted with us. He said, 'I know you, I know Joseph Smith; he was a good man,' and this people are a good people; but the prejudices of the priests and the ungodly are such that, said he, 'Gentlemen, you cannot stay here and live in peace.' We agreed to leave. We left Nauvoo in February, 1846." (*Discourses of Brigham Young* [Salt Lake City: Bookcraft, 1998], p. 473.) ❧

The End of Parley Street,
by Glen S. Hopkinson,
24" x 30",
oil on canvas,
1990

The Journey Begins,
by Glen S. Hopkinson,
60" x 30", oil, 1997

THE JOURNEY BEGINS

*O*ver in England, at the Maritime Museum in Liverpool, I was doing some research for this painting and realized that most people who came to America had to board the ship at Liverpool. I thought of John Cozzens from Wales (my wife's great-grandfather) who boarded the ship S *Curling* in 1856. He crossed the plains with a handcart in the company led by Edward Bunker.

I've read many journal entries of the people who, like John Cozzens, left their homes in England and other places to come to America. It is impossible to catch all of their emotions and feelings in one painting. But I feel that most were coming to America for freedom and hope. They had found the freedom and hope in the gospel and knew that those things could be had in Zion, in America.

Still, there were frequent mentions of father and mother, family and loved ones, left behind as they traveled to Zion. Sister Mary Ann Weston Maughan Davis wrote: "My dear good mother was most brokenhearted to see me go. . . . My two little sisters clung around my neck, saying, 'We shall never see you again.' I had not told them this, for I knew the parting from them would be very hard." (In Richard Neitzel Holzapfel and Jeni Broberg Holzapfel, *Women of Nauvoo* [Salt Lake City: Bookcraft, 1992], p. 2.) ❧

*O*ften working from dawn to dusk, the pioneers ferried their families and possessions across several rivers on their trek west. At times, lines were long for the ferry transportation, but when conditions cooperated, as they did for a time near Fort Laramie at the Platte River, crossings were accomplished quickly—about ten minutes per wagon.

At one point along the trail, the pioneers realized they were ahead of a group of Missourians heading toward California. When the Missourians caught up with the pioneers, they requested help in crossing the Platte. Orson F. Whitney wrote of these pioneers: "At the Black Hills they were seven days in crossing the river. Having there overtaken the Missourians, they ferried them over, also, at the rate of $1.50 for each wagon and load, taking their pay in flour, meal and bacon at Missouri prices. By this time their stock of provisions was well nigh exhausted. To have it thus replenished in the Black Hills, and at the hands of their old enemies, the Missourians, they regarded as little less than a miracle." (In *The Life of Heber C. Kimball* [Salt Lake City: Bookcraft, 1945], pp. 374–75.) ❧

The Morning Breaks, by Glen S. Hopkinson, 30" x 15", oil on canvas, 1983

Pioneer Camp of Israel 1847, by Glen S. Hopkinson, 36" x 24", oil on canvas, 1995

PIONEER CAMP OF ISRAEL 1847

*W*ith determination and faith, the advance, exploratory company of Latter-day Saint pioneers forded swift streams and crossed mountain ranges en route to the Salt Lake Valley. Despite the arduous, 1,032-mile journey, early Saints arrived optimistic and ready to plant their first crops.

These words from Brigham Young describe some of the events along the trail as well as in this painting: "Some of the time we followed Indian trails, some of the time we ran by the compass; when we left the Missouri river we followed the Platte. And we killed rattlesnakes by the cord in some places; and made roads and built bridges till our backs ached. Where we could not build bridges across rivers, we ferried our people across." (*Discourses of Brigham Young* [Salt Lake City: Bookcraft, 1998], p. 480.) ✍

Prove Me Now Herewith, by Glen S. Hopkinson,
40" x 30", oil, 1997

PROVE ME NOW HEREWITH

*F*aithful Saints of all ages learn to trust in the promise of the Lord to Malachi that he will open the windows of heaven to the tithepayer (see Malachi 3:10). During the forty years of sacrifice and effort to build the Salt Lake Temple the tithing office was across the street, where the Joseph Smith Memorial Building now stands. It continued in that location for a few more years after the temple was finished. ❧

WATCHING THE WAGONS

*T*he people who lived in the West when the pioneer movement began, watched the growing influx with many attitudes and feelings. Few understood the depth of change the newcomers would bring. ∾

*Watching the Wagons, by Harold I. Hopkinson,
36" x 24", oil, 1985*

FAITH
HOPE
CHARITY

*A*nd now abideth faith, hope, charity, these three; but the greatest of these is charity" (1 Corinthians 13:13).

As the pioneers crossed the plains, they had to bury many of their own. To depict this I chose as my models a young father, his wife, and their children. We went to the river bottoms, where the father represented a pioneer patriarch who dug a grave as the family looked on. With tear-stained faces the family in this painting clings to each other for security and comfort as they watch a loving sister being buried. This is faith.

To portray hope I chose to paint a handcart pioneer with his family looking to the future and envisioning a better day and the hope that all would be well.

" . . . but the greatest of these is Charity." In the Wyoming Territory a fierce blizzard came suddenly on the hapless handcart pioneers in late October. They were stranded, unprotected from the elements, and starving. Most were too weak to cross the Sweetwater River. It seemed that it would be death itself to step into the freezing river filled with floating chunks of ice. A rescue party was sent from Salt Lake to help. Three of them, eighteen-year-old young men, carried nearly every member of the handcart company across the freezing river. When President Brigham Young heard of this heroic act, he wept like a child and pronounced a wonderful blessing on the heads of C. Allen Huntington, George W. Grant, and David P. Kimball. ∾

Faith, by Harold I. Hopkinson,
40" x 30", oil, 1984

Charity, by Harold I. Hopkinson,
40" x 30", oil, 1984

Hope, by Harold I. Hopkinson,
40" x 30", oil, 1984

*T*he appearance of Jesus Christ in the Americas was the most significant event in the Book of Mormon, since the purpose of the book is to be a second witness of Christ. I have often thought what a marvelous experience it must have been to be one of the few who were privileged to see him and to feel his wounds. ❧

That Ye May Know, by Gary Kapp,
60" x 48", oil, 1996

AMMON IN FRONT OF KING LAMONI

*T*his story from the Book of Mormon demonstrates the fact that sincere love, humility, and the Spirit of the Lord are mightier than the sword in winning the heart of an enemy. These Lamanite people became some of the most faithful members of the Church. Ammon's implicit faith in the Lord has made him one of my personal heroes. ∾

Ammon in Front of King Lamoni, by Gary Kapp, 60" x 48", oil, 1996

ABOUT THE ARTIST

*G*ary Kapp was born in Ogden, Utah. When he was four his father bought a ranch in Oregon, where he was raised until he went to college. He graduated from Brigham Young University with a degree in art in 1966.

After graduation he went to work for a motion picture studio where he spent nearly ten years illustrating film strips, visualizing movies, and painting backdrops. Because his interest in fine art was so intense he left commercial work and began to paint full time.

His work is in collections across the country and is widely shown in major galleries in Arizona, Texas, New Mexico, Colorado, Wyoming, and Utah. He has done several paintings for The Church of Jesus Christ of Latter-day Saints and is currently working on a long-term project to produce twenty-eight paintings depicting Book of Mormon scenes. Gary, his wife, Diane, and their family live in Provo, Utah ∾

The Conversion of Alma the Younger, by Gary Kapp,
96" x 60", oil, 1990

THE CONVERSION OF ALMA THE YOUNGER

*T*his scene is somewhat similar to the experience of Paul in the New Testament. It was not only a profound learning experience for Alma and the sons of Mosiah, but is also one for those who read the account. It was my hope to paint the scene as if the viewer were participating in the event. The figures are near life-size, and as I looked up at the angel while painting Alma, I often felt as though I were actually there. ❧

TEN LEPERS HEALED

Spiritual art is by no means limited to so-called religious subject matter, nor is art with religious subject matter necessarily the fruit of the Spirit. Spiritual art is the result of honest and goodly efforts to reach for an understanding that is beyond our own, hopefully enabling us to better see God. Additional results of this effort, such as increased understanding of ourselves and others, are incidental, even if they are significant.

I rarely paint scriptural imagery. I hope (God is my critic) that I always paint spiritual art, even if it is not obviously so.

Ten Lepers Healed is a painful picture for me for several reasons. The account in the scriptures is, of course, heartbreaking. But as much as I would like to identify with the one grateful, returning beneficiary, I fear I am much more often in the foreground group. It is generally not my practice to anticipate the psychology in the relative placement of the figures, but rather to watch it unfold. This composition unfolded into a "you are here" map—here, in the foreground. Even when we are suitably grateful, the scriptural account is a potent reminder. This painting perhaps suggests one angle from which to observe that reminder. ◦◦

Ten Lepers Healed,
by Brian T. Kershisnik,
42" x 32", oil on board, 1997

ABOUT THE ARTIST

Brian T. Kershisnik was born in Oklahoma City, Oklahoma, on July 6, 1962, the fourth son of good parents. Because of his father's employment as a petroleum geologist, Brian grew up in Luanda, Angola; Bangkok, Thailand; Conroe, Texas; and Islamabad, Pakistan, where he graduated from high school.

After a year of college at the University of Utah, searching in vain for a vocation, he served an LDS mission to Denmark. Following his missionary service he lived with his family in Bergen, Norway, and then returned to the United States to study art at Brigham Young University. During his undergraduate studies he received a grant to study in London for six months. In 1987 he received a bachelor of fine arts degree and married Suzanne Christensen. They moved to Austin, Texas, to pursue a graduate degree. Their first child, Noah, was born in Austin. After his graduate studies at the University of Texas at Austin, Brian and his family moved to Kanosh, a very small town in central Utah, where he paints and works on the house. The family now includes a daughter, Eden, and Iappo, a black dog.

Brian's work is in permanent collections across the country, including the University of Ohio, Illinois State University, Brigham Young University, Delta Airlines, and Nordstrom. ◦◦

David Linn

ASCENT

*T*his painting was created for submission to the LDS Church's Third International Art Competition and Exhibit. I believe the theme for the show was "Living the Gospel in the World Church." My intent was to address what is, for me, at the core of living the gospel. I struggled for quite some time with various concepts when, just at the point of giving up, this image flashed into my mind. I am confident in saying that the idea behind this painting did not originate with me. Inspiration often comes only after we have done our best, exhausted all other possibilities, and are sufficiently humble to be receptive to the Lord's guidance.

I believe that living the gospel requires us to lift one another out of darkness into light. This darkness or opposition can assume many forms, but is an essential element in this mortal probation, as father Lehi taught. As we lift one another we form a living chain on this mountain of mortality and in the process learn those lessons that fit us for the presence of God. ∾

ABOUT THE ARTIST

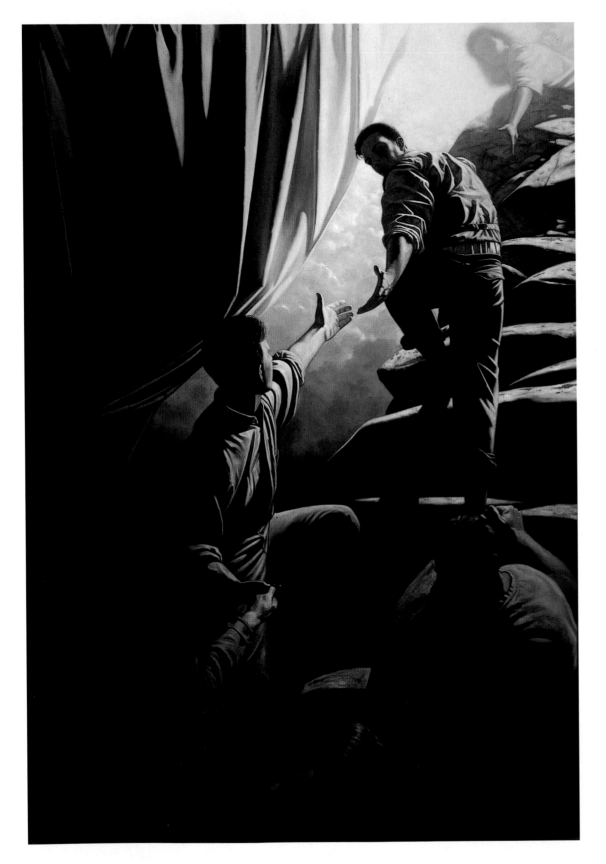

*D*avid Linn was born in Palo Alto, California, and grew up in the beautiful hills of the South Bay peninsula. He began painting shortly after birth and has paused only on rare occasions. He cites influences as divergent as Baroque masters and American Luminists to contemporary conceptual site and earthwork artists. David's work can be found in various museum, corporate, and private collections throughout the country. He graduated from Brigham Young University in 1997 with a master's degree in painting and currently resides in the town of Elk Ridge, Utah. ∾

Ascent, by David Linn, 40" x 60", oil on linen/canvas, 1993

THE CONVERSION OF ALMA THE YOUNGER
AND THE SONS OF MOSIAH

*T*he concepts behind the narrative on which this painting was based have always been, for me, some of the most powerful themes from the Book of Mormon. The story of Alma the younger and the sons of Mosiah deals with mercy, redemption, the omniscience of God, foreordination, submission, and the principles of spiritual rebirth.

I decided a triptych format was most appropriate to suggest the change wrought in the lives of the characters. ✎

The Conversion of Alma the Younger and the Sons of Mosiah, by David Linn, 72" x 48", oil on panel, 1990

Frank Magleby

VALLEY OF ADAM-ONDI-AHMAN

Several years ago, when my wife and I were on our mission, I was discussing some of the Church history sites with a member of the stake presidency in Maryland. He mentioned what a beautiful setting the valley of Adam-ondi-Ahman was, and how impressed he was when he visited it. The Temple Department had asked if I would be willing to do a painting for the St. Louis Temple. Upon visiting this spot on our return to Utah from New England, we found it to be a beautiful pictorial setting with huge oak trees and wild flowers on the hills around the valley. This breathtaking scene in Adam-ondi-Ahman is what I painted for the St. Louis Temple. ❧

Valley of Adam-ondi-Ahman, by Frank Magleby,
48" x 36", oil on panel, 1995

Provo Canyon, by Frank Magleby, 48" x 36",
oil on panel, 1998

PROVO CANYON

$\mathcal{W}$e have a home at Sundance and continually travel through Provo Canyon, never tiring of its beauty. One day in early fall it was particularly beautiful with the autumn colors reflecting in the water of the Provo River and the majestic cliffs in the hazy evening light warming the background. I knew immediately that it was a painting waiting to be created. ❧

Village of Downham, by Frank Magleby, 40" x 30", oil on panel, 1995

VILLAGE OF DOWNHAM

Downham, England, is a village rich in early Church history. It is much the same today as it appeared in 1837 and 1838 when Heber C. Kimball and Joseph Fielding converted many in the village. When they left this area and walked down the road with tears in their eyes as they bade farewell to the Saints, the little children followed them, singing Church hymns. They were so touched by the experience that Elder Fielding wrote, "It was very affecting to witness our parting with them. The streets were almost lined with people, weeping and looking after us. Brother Kimball left his blessing on them and the whole place, walking with his hat off. They all followed us with their eyes as far as they could see us, many of those even that had not been baptized." When Elder Kimball recounted this story to Joseph Smith on his return home from England the Prophet told Heber C. Kimball that ancient prophets walked those roads and blessed that land. Their blessings had fallen upon him. ❧

SUSQUEHANNA RIVER

*T*he site where the priesthood was restored and the first baptisms performed was an important historical subject for me to paint. The day my wife and I arrived to get material for the painting, we discovered a group of young missionaries from Harrisburg, Pennsylvania, with their mission president holding a retreat. In discussing the site with the mission president, he mentioned that when President Spencer W. Kimball was visiting this site, he had a strong impression that the area I planned to paint was the exact location where John the Baptist appeared and the baptisms were performed. The Spirit still permeates this area, and you feel it very strongly when you are there. ❧

Susquehanna River,
by Frank Magleby,
40" x 30",
oil on panel,
1995

Sacred Grove

My wife and I arrived in Palmyra as part of our Church service mission in the early morning on a late spring day and were later alone in the sacred grove. It was so peaceful and quiet, except for the birds singing and the bees humming, we felt that it must have been much as it was so many years ago when a young boy went into the grove to pray for guidance. This scene was the impetus for *Sacred Grove*, which the members in our ward in Vermont felt should hang in "their" temple in Boston. The painting will be hung in the Boston temple upon the temple's completion.

Sacred Grove, by Frank Magleby, 48" x 36", oil on panel, 1995

*Skenfrith,
by Frank Magleby,
48" x 36",
oil on panel,
1995*

*T*his is a scene from a tiny village in eastern Wales that caught my eye as we crossed over the bridge spanning the Monnow River in Skenfrith. The view toward the bridge was especially beautiful, and after wandering on the banks I envisioned a painting that would be appropriate for the temple. Some weeks later I was reading in our reference book, *Truth Will Prevail,* and discovered that some of the earliest converts in Wales were baptized in the Monnow River in Skenfrith. ∾

ABOUT THE ARTIST

*F*rancis R. (Frank) Magleby was born in Idaho and spent his early years there in a rural community where his father was a schoolteacher and rancher. His family moved to Portland, Oregon, when he was six years old. Early on he was recognized as an artist. Among the honors he received as a young man was a scholarship to the Portland Art Museum School.

He attended Brigham Young University on a football scholarship, majored in art, received a bachelor's degree in 1950 and a master's degree in 1952.

As an army photographer in Europe from 1952 to 1954, Frank had the opportunity to study great works of art in Italy and throughout Europe. Returning from abroad, he studied at the American Art School and Art Students League in New York City.

In 1959, Frank welcomed a chance to return west and accept a faculty position at BYU. From 1965 through 1968 he served as the director of the B. F. Larsen gallery on the BYU campus. He completed his doctorate in art education from Columbia University in 1967. He retired in 1990, after more than three decades at BYU.

His paintings hang in public and private collections throughout the United States, including many works purchased by The Church of Jesus Christ of Latter-day Saints for exhibition in its offices, museums, and temples.

In April of 1994, he and his wife began a service mission for the LDS Church. The mission entailed eighteen months of travel throughout the United States, Great Britain, and China, completing paintings commissioned by the Church. He completed twenty-four paintings for temples, including the following: Hong Kong; London and Preston, England; Orlando, Florida; San Diego; Boston; White Plains, New York; Nashville; St. Louis; Mount Timpanogos; and others not yet determined.

At present, he divides his time between his homes in Vermont and Utah, as both places have the material he most loves to paint. ∾

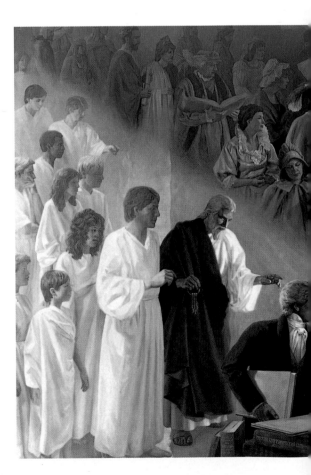

The Eternal Family Through Christ, by Judith Mehr, 23' x 7', oil on canvas, 1985-1988

THE ETERNAL FAMILY THROUGH CHRIST

Judith Mehr

*T*here are seventy-four figures in the mural representing various phases of life. The overall compositional structure has Jesus Christ positioned on the pivotal "golden section" (about one third of the distance from the right edge). This proportion historically has been used to feature the most important aspect of the composition because of its inherent strength and eye appeal. The rest of the composition is designed to facilitate the flow of the story and give an overall geometric solidity and strength to the concepts.

The painting illustrates the plan of salvation and theme of family togetherness throughout all the phases of life:

First, on the left side, are individuals in the spirit world before they are born. They press forward, anticipating the experiences of mortality.

Above and to the right of the spirit world, descending in a triangular shape, are deceased ancestors from Adam and Eve, on down. Some are reaching out to the contemporary family in an effort to form lasting relationships and inspire the contemporary family to remember them.

Under the triangle of ancestors is a figure representing the prophet Elijah, who holds the symbolic priesthood keys to the Restoration. He is symbolically reaching out his other hand to confer this power and admonition on the figure representing Joseph Smith.

Near the figure of Joseph Smith are books representing family histories that Joseph then shares as a mission and vision of humanity with a contemporary family.

In the center-left, the contemporary family is gathered together remembering their relatives. Influenced by the mission of Elijah and Joseph Smith, they develop an appreciation for their ancestral heritage.

Jesus Christ is the focal point of the mural, and the figure representing him is framed in a mandorla, an art-historical device formed at the juncture of two intersecting circles. The two circles represent heaven and earth, and Christ bridges the two as does the temple depicted behind him.

On the right side are the followers of the Lord's plan. They represent family groups that have passed on to the next life and are able to be together, progressing in knowledge, experience, happiness, and truth. ❧

Moses and the Brazen Serpent

Warren Luch commissioned me on behalf of the Church Educational System to illustrate the scene in the Old Testament where Moses raises up an image of a serpent for the people to look upon and be healed from their afflictions. This story is, of course, symbolic of Jesus Christ being lifted up on the cross and saving us from our sins if we would accept him. Warren worked with me as art director on the design and style of this piece. I used friends and family members as models and borrowed the Old World clothing from the LDS Motion Pictures Studio. We wanted the painting to have a classical, "old-masters" feel to it, so I painted it in a controlled, highly finished style with dramatic backlighting. The brazen serpent, backlit by the rising sun, is centered for maximum effect as the focal point of the painting—a focal point that foreshadows Jesus' sacrifice on the cross. ❧

Moses and the Brazen Serpent,
by Judith Mehr, 26" x 40",
oil on canvas, 1996

Ruth & Naomi

Warren Luch of the Church graphics department commissioned me on behalf of the Relief Society General Board to do a painting that would be hung in the Relief Society boardroom illustrating the theme "Charity Never Faileth." He consulted with me on the design, style, and execution of the painting. We wanted to create a scene depicting the love and charity Ruth and Naomi shared with each other by illustrating a scene in which Naomi brings water to a hot and thirsty Ruth, who is gleaning wheat in the fields of Boaz.

I used my good friends Linda Gibbs and her mother-in-law, Katherine Gibbs, as the models for the painting. The expression of love and gratitude on Ruth's face exhibits that quality of tenderness between the two that we wanted to illustrate. The painting is done in a modified impressionist style to compliment the texture of the wheat and the light, open field. ❧

Ruth and Naomi, by Judith Mehr,
58" x 43", oil on canvas, 1992

*J*udith Mehr was born May 5, 1951, in San Francisco, California. In 1969 she received an art scholarship to Brigham Young University and graduated with a bachelor of fine arts degree in 1974. After a year of graduate school, Judith returned to California and began working on an active art career.

In 1978, Judith moved from California to Salt Lake City, Utah, to continue her art career and pursue illustration and portrait commissions received from the LDS Church and other private and corporate clients in Utah. She began to achieve a reputation as a fine portrait artist and genre-scene painter, and has exhibited oil and watercolor landscapes, still lifes, and genre-scenes in galleries and arts festivals. Judith continues to be highly active in art creation and exhibition in Utah. She has also done work for government, corporate, and individual collections in the western and southern United States, Pennsylvania, New York, and Japan.

In 1991, while still painting commissions and exhibition work in galleries of the type for which she was known, Judith began to change the visualization of content for her painting. Instead of painting in a straight, representational manner as before, she began to experiment with combining realistic and abstract images in a more interpretive and intuitive manner. She is currently exhibiting these new works in various juried shows and galleries. These new images are receiving positive responses from art critics, clients, and peers. ❧

O JERUSALEM

"*O* Jerusalem, Jerusalem . . . how often would I have gathered thy children together, even as a hen gathereth her chickens under her wings" (Matthew 23:37). This is a Messianic exclamation of profound concern and unconditional love for all who have lost their way and suffer while wandering in spiritual darkness. As the slanting rays of the sun reflect upon the rooftops of Old Jerusalem, Christ reflects upon his life's mission and upon those he came to serve and bless. His gaze takes in the glistening gold and marble of Herod's temple and the smoke of burnt offerings upon the altar.

He was keenly aware that soon he would offer himself up as the true Passover Lamb—"the Lamb of God." Here, upon the Mount of Olives, Jesus could see the day, like his mortal ministry, coming to a close. However, a new day always dawns, and there is hope and comfort in his words, "lo, I am with you always" (Matthew 28:20). Just as he looked down upon the traveling pilgrims entering Jerusalem, he watches still from yet a higher vantage point, ready to extend his protective wing to all who seek him. ∾

O Jerusalem, © Greg Olsen, 50" x 36", oil on canvas, 1995

ABOUT THE ARTIST

*B*orn in 1958, Greg Olsen was raised in a farming community in rural Idaho. His parents, artists themselves, recognized and encouraged his early love of drawing. Later, the devoted tutelage of a high school teacher cemented his affinity and enhanced his technical ability. After studying illustration at Utah State University, he was hired as an in-house illustrator in Salt Lake City, working on anything from murals and dioramas to simple paste-up. Two years later he followed a friend's advice and began painting full time.

His Biblical paintings, represented in religious temples in more than twenty countries around the world, and his work for the Pentagon and the National Collegiate Athletic Association require intensive research and strict attention to factual detail. While these historical paintings satisfy his desire to render works with a sense of permanence, his whimsical paintings afford him the freedom to transfer his imagination to canvas. When Olsen paints a tree house, he paints it the way the children climbing into it imagine it to be—the simple boards and nails of reality become elaborate, majestic castles in the sky.

Olsen's philosophy on art is quite simple. "For me, I just always appreciated the beauty of art and the way it made me feel," he says. "Art's greatest purpose it just to make us happy. I take a lot of pleasure in painting and hope that pleasure is contagious to those who look at my art." ∾

Artwork by Greg Olsen courtesy of the artist and Mill Pond Press, Inc., Venice, Florida 34292

Winter Quarters, © Greg Olsen, 56" x 22",
oil on canvas, 1997

WINTER QUARTERS

*T*he indomitable human spirit is exemplified by the early pioneers of the American frontier who, in times of great adversity, turned suffering and hardship into opportunities for growth and experience. The external conditions weathered by these pioneers were often harsh, and winter's severity forced them to take refuge in temporary settlements referred to by trappers and explorers as "winter quarters."

Within the confines of this shelter, however, tragedy was no stranger. When disease struck, it took a heavy toll, and hundreds would succumb, weakened by inadequate provisions and fatigue.

Fortunately this austere existence did not crowd out of life the joy of living. Laughter, merriment, playfulness, the lively strains of the violin, and the dancing party were still observed. Music and song nowhere and at no time better served their purpose of cheering the hearts of men than in these wilderness encampments. ❧

LOST NO MORE

*T*he shepherd and his flock have been ever-present symbols of the Lord and the people of his pasture. The ancient role of a shepherd was much more than an assignment to herd sheep. The shepherd loved his sheep; he knew them, named them, provided for, and protected them. In return, the sheep responded to their shepherd and recognized his voice. His call alone could bring them back from their wanderings in unfamiliar paths. If lambs were lost, he sought them out and brought them back to the fold.

Those that hear the Master's call and then seek to follow in his path will find him and there enjoy contentment and safety at his feet. ❧

Lost No More, © Greg Olsen, 30" x 40", oil on canvas, 1997

FOREVER AND EVER

Surrounded by the Savior's enduring love, we are warm, safe, and secure. That reassuring calm comes not from a spoken word or by gazing with our eyes upon his strong arms. It comes from the embrace which our heart feels and through the tender senses of our spirit. All around us we have the physical wonders and beauties of nature that bear the signature of their Creator and remind us of his enduring love. Although his presence is unseen by our eyes, his unending love is felt in our hearts. ❧

Forever and Ever, © Greg Olsen,
24" x 30", oil on canvas, 1997

SACRED GROVE

*T*he shady cathedral of the woods has long offered a retreat to the soul seeking communion with nature and her Creator. The trees rise like mighty spires, lifting our gaze and our thoughts heavenward. Layers of leaves are illuminated like a stained glass window as the morning sun filters through them. The delicate notes of songbirds float like a hymn upon the still air. Rays of light stream down from the windows of heaven, warming the forest floor below. They rest upon one's being and take away the chill of darker hours. It is in quiet places and in simple ways that heaven's veil is parted for those who knock upon its door. ❧

Sacred Grove, © Greg Olsen, 48" x 24", oil on canvas, 1991

THE GOOD SHEPHERD

*T*he age-old symbol of the Good Shepherd has brought peace and comfort to the hearts of many throughout the years. The strong and watchful keeper of the flock, who knows his sheep and is known by them, guides the sheep to green pastures and to still waters where they can graze and safely drink. He gathers them before the approaching storm and searches for those that may be lost. He places himself between danger and the flock he tends. His sheep recognize his voice, and his call is a call to peace, safety, and contentment. ❧

The Good Shepherd, © Greg Olsen,
16" x 20", oil on canvas, 1995

The Reason for the Season,
© Greg Olsen,
48" x 36",
oil on canvas,
1995

THE REASON FOR THE SEASON

$\mathcal{E}$nter a wonderland where twinkling lights shine on an array of symbols of the season. From attic hideaways come holiday treasures to cast their spells over the young at heart. The boxes and bows, tinsel and trim wrap you in a warm, cozy spirit. The ribbons and reindeer, the soldiers and trains turn your mind back to the storefront windows and you can almost imagine your nose pressed against the cold, frosty glass. Reminders of Santa and sleigh rides, falling snow and shining stars bring back the excitement of a sleepless December night. Nuzzle a fuzzy teddy bear and hear the sound of a jingling bell or a glistening golden horn. Put yourself into the miniature worlds of a Dickens village and stroll the winter streets with the shoppers and carolers. Toylike angel dolls and little snare drums are found beneath the fragrant evergreen. The wafting scent of pine boughs carries you to a magical place called Christmas. All these things form the accessories of the season, the decorations that lift and cheer us, but they only reflect the light of that which shines most brightly: a humble couple and a tiny babe, lying in a manger—the true meaning of Christmas—the reason for the season! ❧

BE NOT AFRAID

*L*ike children who have lost their way
Alone and comfortless we wander.
Stumbling through woods that grow deep and ever darker,
With no direction, we cry for help
And hear our pleas echo through the canyons.
Is there anyone who can hear us?
Then, like a rushing wind, a voice whispers to our hearts.
And through tear-filled eyes, we see an outstretched hand,
There to lead us home.
Though swirling streams may block our way
And slippery stones betray our feet,
He leads us on. He knows the way, His feet are sure,
And in Him we find safe passage. ☙

IN HIS CONSTANT CARE

*P*erhaps no other being in history has been the subject of more artwork than that of Christ. Artistic masters throughout the ages have been drawn to the challenge of portraying themes of inspiration and significance. The life of Christ is an enduring model of humility, compassion, and love.

This painting is a visual reminder of one of his most comforting messages regarding the worth of each individual soul. "Are not five sparrows sold for two farthings, and not one of them is forgotten before God? But even the very hairs of your head are all numbered. Fear not therefore: ye are of more value than many sparrows." (Luke 12:6–7.)

As I look at the intricate design of these little sparrows, experience tells me that where there is a design, there is a designer! It is a comforting thought to consider that somewhere there is a Creator who is aware of and has love for even the least of his creations. There is incredible intimacy in the vastness of this thought. ❧

In His Constant Care, © Greg Olsen, 32" x 48", oil on canvas, 1992

Wilson Jay Ong

GOOD SAMARITAN

I was very interested in the emotions that the lines created in the painting. The Samaritan is strong and very straight in pose, while the state of the poor victim is determined by the detail and confusion of the lines of his gesture. I enjoyed the contrast of these lines as they communicated emotions that transcend literal perceptions. In addition, the donkey is a shadow over the Samaritan, and as it looks down toward the fallen man, a look of pathos and care are etched in its eyes. The primary design of the piece is triangular, giving it the timeless quality of traditional paintings from the past. The lighting and mood of the painting are somber and direct, adding to the significance of the moment and event. ❧

Good Samaritan, by Wilson Jay Ong,
24" x 36", oil on canvas, 1986

GENESIS OF REPENTANCE

*T*his painting was inspired by the principle that repentance begins first through the realization of one's sins. I wanted to create an image that showed the prodigal son grappling with this and thus beginning his road to repentance. The painting takes a number of liberties, but is distilled to the most important elements. Therefore the look on the young man's face and the pigs became ingredients to this work. Of interest is the young man who posed for this painting. His family are my neighbors, and I had known their son as a friend and a youth leader. Between the time I created this painting and a couple of years after, I watched this young friend literally become a prodigal son. After falling into the darker side of life, he one day made a turn and painstakingly changed his ways and eventually served an honorable full-time mission and married in the temple. ❧

Genesis of Repentance, by Wilson Jay Ong,
30" x 40", oil on canvas, 1992

ABOUT THE ARTIST

*W*ilson Jay Ong was born November 8, 1958, in Oakland, California, to Chinese emigrants James and Jane Ong. He was raised in Hayward, California, and attended school there until he came to Utah to attend Brigham Young University. He was baptized on April 15, 1977, while attending BYU. He then served a full-time mission to Nagoya, Japan, from 1978 to 1980. He received a bachelor of fine arts degree in painting from BYU in 1982, after which he attended the Art Students' League in New York City.

Wilson has worked as a professional artist since 1983 and is presently teaching art at the Waterford School in Sandy, Utah.

Wilson and his wife, Mannie, have three daughters: Tatum, Anna, and Jemi. ∿

Elder Neal A. Maxwell, by Wilson Jay Ong, 22" x 28", oil on canvas, 1990

ELDER NEAL A. MAXWELL

I did this portrait for the Museum of Church History and Art. I was excited to do this portrait and meet this man of God, whom I had seen and heard of so much. I was impressed by his gentleness and unassuming character. As part of the creative process I asked him a number of questions and did a number of sketches. Elder Maxwell pointed out how important it was for him to be a good listener. This particular quality was a natural part of him, and thus the design and mood of the portrait followed. ∿

Del Parson

STORYTIME IN GALILEE

Christ told the little children to "come unto me." *Storytime in Galilee* is a depiction of this happy and positive event. The main thing I wanted to express was Christ's love for children. Through his parables we are aware of his keen observations of nature and natural events. I wanted to show the area where he walked and observed his creations, such as Galilee in springtime, covered with red lilies of the field. ❧

Storytime in Galilee, by Del Parson, 72" x 60", oil, 1996

THE SAVIOR

The Savior portrays a gentle, loving, and kind Savior. I did a similar painting years ago that was very masculine, authoritative, and strong. Here I wanted to have a different feeling conveyed. In this painting I love the feelings of acceptance expressed. ✺

The Savior, by Del Parson,
14" x 18", oil, 1995

ABOUT THE ARTIST

*B*orn in Ogden, Utah, in 1948, Del Parson has been drawing and painting since he was a child. Del received formal training in art at Ricks College and Brigham Young University, where he was awarded his bachelor's degree in 1972 and master of fine arts degree in 1975. He has painted professionally for twenty-three years and is in his tenth year of teaching, currently an associate professor at Dixie College.

Del continues to produce art for a variety of private and corporate collections. ✺

THE FIRST VISION

*T*he purpose of *The First Vision* was to portray the glory of the Father and the Son and their love for us in appearing to Joseph Smith. In this painting I wanted to show that it was a real event and paint it as it was viewed through the eyes of the young Joseph Smith. ∾

The First Vision, by Del Parson,
30" x 40", oil, 1988

THE LOST SHEEP

*T*he parable of the lost sheep reminds me of the importance of the individual. I wanted to portray a tender scene of the Shepherd lovingly returning the lost one to the fold. ❧

The Lost Sheep, by Del Parson,
28" x 22", oil, 1990

THE GREATEST OF ALL
(Christ in Gethsemane)

*O*riginally, I wanted to show the real suffering of Christ in *The Greatest of All*. But I could not paint the pain he suffered more than any man. What I showed instead was his triumph over the suffering. ❧

The Greatest of All, by Del Parson,
30" x 40", oil, 1989

HE IS RISEN

*T*he greatest event in the history of the world was the atonement and resurrection of Jesus Christ. I wanted to paint the garden tomb where many believed this great event occurred, and capture Christ's first step from the tomb, with his realization that he had accomplished all that the Father had wanted. *He Is Risen* gives us hope and reminds us that all will triumph over death. ◌

He Is Risen, by Del Parson,
30" x 40", oil, 1996

BEHOLD YOUR LITTLE ONES

*M*y favorite scripture is 3 Nephi 17. I love to read about Christ's appearance to the Nephites and his great love for people. *Behold Your Little Ones* was commissioned by the LDS Church. They requested that the children be Mesoamerican. I tried to depict it just as the scriptures said, filled with the light of fire and angels. ∾

Behold Your Little Ones,
by Del Parson,
30" x 40",
oil, 1995

Clark Kelley Price

SHALL WE NOT GO ON IN SO GREAT A CAUSE?

I did this painting for the international Church art competition. I had prayed for help to know what I should paint, and I received an answer. This painting is the result. I saw this whole scene in my mind's eye. I could see the Saints struggling in the mud with their shoulders to the wheel. I could see the spirit of the Prophet Joseph beckoning them on. It sent chills up my back. I knew I needed to paint it. The help given me was not of this world. ∞

Shall We Not Go on in So Great a Cause?, by Clark Kelley Price, 40" x 30", oil on canvas, 1991

Trail of Sacrifice—Valley of Promise, by Clark Kelley Price,
20" x 16", oil on canvas, 1995

TRAIL OF SACRIFICE—VALLEY OF PROMISE

I painted this scene to express the many emotions of the pioneers as they gained their first view of the Valley.

The trail had been hard and long from Winter Quarters to the Valley of Promise, and many had followed an even longer trail from the old country. Their sacrifices along the way are unnumbered and cannot be told completely but, I hope, can be seen in their faces and their bodies.

We face many challenges today and must point our faces toward the promised land as well. We can take courage from them and their examples and, in turn, walk the trail that lies before us with the same spirit they possessed. We too must leave a great legacy of faith in Jesus Christ, a heritage of courage in the gospel to those who follow us. ℘

WHEN THE ANGELS COME

*T*his painting was commissioned by the *Ensign* magazine. The story behind it comes from an address by President David O. McKay given at an annual Relief Society conference in 1947, the centennial year of the Saints' arrival in the Valley.

In that address, President McKay talked of the criticism given by a teacher who commented to his class that it was very unwise to have even permitted the Saints to cross the plains under such circumstances as did the Willie and Martin Handcart Companies. President McKay said:

"Some sharp criticism of the Church and its leaders was being indulged in for permitting any company of converts to venture across the plains with no more supplies or protection than a handcart caravan afforded.

"An old man [Francis Webster] in the corner sat silent and listened as long as he could stand it, then he arose and said things that no person who heard him will ever forget. His face was white with emotion, yet he spoke calmly, deliberately, but with great earnestness and sincerity.

"In substance [he] said, 'I ask you to stop this criticism. You are discussing a matter you know nothing about. Cold historic facts mean nothing here, for they give no proper interpretation of the questions involved. Mistake to send the handcart company out so late in the season? Yes. But I was in that company and my wife was in it and Sister Nellie Unthank whom you have cited was there too. We suffered beyond anything you can imagine, and many died of exposure and starvation, but did you ever hear a survivor of that company utter a word of criticism? Not one of that company ever apostatized or left the Church, because everyone of us came through with the absolute knowledge that God lives, for we became acquainted with him in our extremities.

"'I have pulled my handcart when I was so weak and weary from illness and lack of food that I could hardly put one foot ahead of the other. I have looked ahead and seen a patch of sand or a hill slope, and I have said, I can go only that far and there I must give up, for I cannot pull the load through it. I have gone on to that sand and when I reached it, the cart began pushing me. I have looked back many times to see who was pushing my cart, but my eyes saw no one. I knew then that the angels of God were there.

"'Was I sorry that I chose to come by handcart? No. Neither then nor any minute of my life since. The price we paid to become acquainted with God was a privilege to pay, and I am thankful that I was privileged to come in the Martin handcart company.'" (In "The Cart Began Pushing Me," *Relief Society Magazine*, January 1948, p. 8.) ❧

When the Angels Come, by Clark Kelley Price,
40" x 30", oil on canvas, 1992

First Missionaries to Samoa, by Clark Kelley Price,
36" x 24", oil on canvas, 1990

FIRST MISSIONARIES TO SAMOA

I was commissioned by the Church through Emil Fetzer, the Church architect, to do this painting for the temple in Samoa. It depicts the arrival of Joseph Dean, his wife, Florence, and child to the small island of Aunu'u on June 21, 1888. The man without a hand, helping carry the trunk ashore, actually had been doing missionary work there years earlier and was also one of the first missionaries to Samoa. ❧

Fishers of Men,
by Clark Kelley Price,
36" x 24", oil on canvas, 1979

FISHERS OF MEN

I was blessed to have two wonderful mission presidents: Patrick D. Dalton at the first of my mission and John H. Groberg at the end. President Groberg commissioned me to do this painting of our mission (the Tongan Mission), and depict two young Tongan Elders just arriving on an island with all their possessions rolled up in the mats they are carrying. As shown here, some of the Tongan elders resisted ties and shirts buttoned at the neck and purposely removed the top button of their shirts to allow more freedom. But these elders were some of the Lord's most powerful servants, faithful under all hardships.

I can still see two of those elders in my mind's eye. I met them in Pangai when I was on a transfer to the island of Niue. They had strong bronze bodies, beautiful white teeth, and confident smiles. They stood side by side, almost identical in appearance, holding their scriptures, secure in their special kind of Tongan faith. These simple and pure servants of the Lord, and many more like them have helped literally to change the face of a nation from shadowy darkness to the brilliant light of Christ. A temple of the Lord now stands there as a symbol of it! ∾

ARRIVAL IN THE PROMISED LAND

I did this painting at the request of a great lady in my ward. She has since passed away, but her son-in-law has the painting hanging in his dental office for all to see and receive of its message. Because of this, many nonmembers of the Church have asked the meaning of the painting and learned more about the Book of Mormon. ∾

Arrival in the Promised Land, by Clark Kelley Price,
24" x 18", oil on canvas, 1988

NEPHI'S VISION

I was commissioned to do a series of paintings from the Book of Mormon. This particular scene was done to bring us close to the young Nephi and to feel the Lord's power upon him. It helps us know that we too can be like Nephi of old. We too can say, "I will go and do the things which the Lord hath commanded" (1 Nephi 3:7). Men like Nephi did not set themselves above the rest, but rather they were humble and invited all to walk the path they walked—to walk side by side with them. ∾

Nephi's Vision, by Clark Kelley Price,
24" x 36", oil on canvas, 1980

THE LORD FULFILLETH ALL HIS WORDS

*A*t the time I did this painting I was quite concerned about world conditions, prophecies of the last days, and the need to prepare. It seemed to me that Noah had had a message for all of us. He *was* prepared. He had tried so hard to help the people avert catastrophe, but they didn't take him seriously. The lion roars at the disobedient people, giving them a message: "Even we animals are obedient to God. Why aren't you?" This painting is an image from older times, but it asks the same question of us today as Noah did in his time: "Are you prepared, are you obeying the prophets' counsel and warning?" The answer is the same today as well: If not, you will be swept away by floods of sin and deception; your spirit will sink to destruction. ༄

The Lord Fulfilleth All His Words, by Clark Kelley Price,
40" x 30", oil on canvas, 1987

DAN JONES AWAKENS WALES

*T*his painting was commissioned by the Sons of the Utah Pioneers to be given as a gift to the Church, specifically to be hung in the Missionary Training Center. I received much help from Carma De Jong Anderson, an expert in clothing of the period right before the martyrdom of the Prophet.

Dan Jones was with the Prophet in the Carthage Jail and he felt he too would die. But Joseph put his hand on Dan's shoulder and prophesied "you will live to see Wales and fill your mission there." Dan Jones was fearless and effective in Wales, overcoming great opposition and bringing thousands into the Church. ༄

ABOUT THE ARTIST

Clark Kelley Price was born in Idaho Falls, Idaho, in 1945. As a child he loved to draw. His parents recognized his talent and encouraged him to use it. He received his formal education at Ricks College and Brigham Young University; however, his deep commitment to the gospel, his love of the West—both modern and historic—and his life experiences have been his greatest resources in developing his talent.

Clark served an LDS mission to the Tongan Mission, in the Fiji Islands District from 1964 to 1966. Missionary work has continued to be a vital part of his life. He states that he "would not sit down and start painting without asking the Lord to help me, for He is the one who gave me this talent." Clark is committed to using his talent to help build up God's kingdom. Stories from the Bible, the

Book of Mormon, and Church history have become more vivid and personal through his art. The spiritual impact of his religious paintings makes his work outstanding. As an example, he is a direct descendant of members of the Martin Handcart Company and has profound personal feelings for their hardships. His depiction of pioneer experiences such as burying their dead in icy graves and having angels walk alongside them deeply impacts those who view his artwork.

He has painted full-time since 1973. The *Ensign* magazine often uses his work, and he has done paintings for temples in Tonga, Samoa, and Seattle, as well as for the MTC in Provo. He has illustrated several books and book covers.

He and his wife, Irene, reside in Star Valley, Wyoming. They are the parents of seven children. ✎

Dan Jones Awakens Wales,
by Clark Kelley Price,
48" x 36", oil on canvas, 1993

Ron Richmond

OLD COMPASS—NEW STAR

I believe in the emotional power of the arts, whether positive or negative. I am an idealist and am concerned with the potential that art has for the good. The negative in our world is obvious and ubiquitous; it is tiresomely exploited and constantly confronts our awareness in the arts. Art with a message of hope, peace, and faith is what I want to create.

In some paintings I use collaged maps to represent guides for our life journeys. We use maps, guides, and charts—literally and figuratively—to navigate our way through life, finding solace along the way in the peaceful and the sublime.

This particular painting, titled *old compass—new star*, refers to the new star that appeared at the birth of Christ and was a guide for those who wanted to see the child. For centuries, Polaris, or the North Star, has been used as a fixed point on which to navigate. The compass typifies the gospel that guides us in this life. ✎

old compass—new star, by Ron Richmond,
22-1/2" x 35-5/8", oil, collage on board, 1996

ABOUT THE ARTIST

*R*on Richmond was born in Denver, Colorado, in 1963. He served a mission for the LDS Church in Rosario, Argentina, and then attended school at Brigham Young University in Provo, Utah, where he graduated with a master's degree in fine art.

The majority of his life had been spent in big cities until 1995 when he moved with his family to rural Sanpete County, Utah. He lives in Mt. Pleasant with his wife, Vicki, his daughter, Brette, and two sons, Jesse and Max. He paints in a studio in a historic building on Mt. Pleasant's Main Street.

Ron has been painting professionally since 1992. His artwork is on display in galleries across the country in San Francisco, Pam Desert, Park City, Salt Lake City, Houston, Atlanta, and New Orleans. He completed a large commission in 1996 for Saks Fifth Avenue.

He won first place at the Mormon Arts Festival in Tuacahn, Utah, in 1998. He has twice been a finalist in the Utah Arts Council's fellowship competition. His artwork can be found in *Utah Painting and Sculpture* (Swanson, Olpin, Seifrit, Salt Lake City: Gibbs Smith, 1997). ✎

MY FATHER'S HOUSE

*T*his is my interpretation of the Garden of Gethsemane on the afternoon of the Atonement. I researched this painting carefully. I not only wanted it to be archaeologically correct as far as the city was concerned, but the garden also. The fruit, nuts, and herbs would have been in bloom in early April. The view of the city is from the Orson Hyde Gardens. My feeling is that the Savior would have wanted to see the temple and view the splendor of Jerusalem. ✑

My Father's House, by Al Rounds, 36" x 23", watercolor, 1993

Manti, by Al Rounds, 22" x 16", watercolor, 1986

MANTI

$\mathcal{T}$his painting was found through the rearview mirror of my car. My daughter Quinn and I had spent all day in Manti looking for something to paint. As we were leaving Manti, just at dusk, I looked in my rearview mirror, and there it was, the perfect picture to paint. ❧

McKay Home, Huntsville

*T*he white Huntsville, Utah, house on the left, surrounded by lilacs, is the boyhood home of President David O. McKay, who was born the eighth day of September 1873. He was ordained to the Quorum of the Twelve Apostles on April 9, 1906, and as President of the Church on April 9, 1951. He died the eighteenth day of January 1970, at age ninety-six. As the prophet of my boyhood, President McKay had always been my hero. Standing by his boyhood home, I could picture him as a young boy climbing trees, riding horses, and cleaning irrigation ditches. That brought a new connection of heroism to my dashing remembrance of him. ⌘

McKay Home, Huntsville, by Al Rounds, 25-1/2" x 20", watercolor, 1995

HEBER C. KIMBALL HOME

*T*he Heber C. Kimball home in Nauvoo, shown with the Nauvoo Temple in the background, was erected in 1845. The Kimball family lived there for only five months. Unable to sell their home before their departure from Nauvoo, they abandoned it on the fourth of February 1846, to make the trek west. Today the home is one of numerous homes visited by tourists in Nauvoo.

Dr. J. LeRoy Kimball, who started Nauvoo restoration with the purchase of his grandfather's house, lent his car to us while we were there. The streets were so frozen that when you shut the car door, the whole car would slide. That particular year the Mississippi froze over completely. The days were between 30 and 60 degrees below zero. As I stood in the fields of Nauvoo trying to find something to paint, only the tip of my nose poked out from my covering. In moments it would start to hurt from the cold. My camera would not function, so I kept it beneath my clothes until the last possible moment. All these things were insignificant to the suffering of the Saints, but it certainly made me aware of even the extreme hardships that were born by the miracle of the freezing over of the great Mississippi River in 1845. ❧

Heber C. Kimball Home, by Al Rounds,
24" x 16", watercolor, 1980

Jordan River Temple

Living in Sandy at the time, the Jordan River Temple was my family's temple. We raised money, took pictures of the construction, and sang in the choir at the dedication. But my spot was on the hill to the east, just below the railroad tracks and overlooking the Jordan River Valley, right on the edge of the old irrigation ditch. Spring, summer, fall, and winter I would stop and check it out. Then one afternoon in late winter, there it was, the painting that fit my feelings. ❧

Jordan River Temple, by Al Rounds, 42" x 34", watercolor, 1983

About the Artist

Al Rounds's transparent watercolors register a beautiful familiarity with the world we all love. They carry us over a distance of miles and years, which speak of history revisited and of lives well lived.

Scouring backroads and country lanes, searching for the past, Al Rounds continues to capture a particular reverence for the pride of a place. Travel provides an ongoing source of inspiration for Al. Some of his favorite findings are in up-state New York with its rural integrity and four-season beauty, in England with its meandering, damp cobblestone streets, and in the pioneer history that still crowds the fence lines and farmsteads of his native Utah.

The size, historical significance, and accuracy of the architectural landscapes he creates are hallmarks of his work. Al can't think of a time when he didn't want to be an artist. While his classmates were working on the serious business of school, Al would be gazing out the window, daydreaming about drawing. It's apparent he has always been drawn to architectural landscape. His first grade teacher sent a note home to his mother asking if Al knew how to draw anything other than his house.

In 1977 he earned his bachelor's degree from the University of Utah. His painting technique was influenced there by the English portrait master, Alvin Gittings, and newspaper art critic and watercolorist, George Dibble.

Utah-born, Al Rounds was brought up in the small-town community of Walnut Creek, California. He now finds retreat in his home nestled in the Rocky Mountains of Utah. His wife and seven children are welcome and enthusiastic visitors to his studio located at their home. ❧

TAKEN IN ADULTERY

*T*his work is a religious affirmation; it adheres to a belief, professes a faith, and aspires to the lofty goal of conveying truth—truth that exists independently of artistic concerns. Nevertheless, this truth is placed into the magic matrix of color and form, harbored in the aesthetic ambience of art. Art, in turn, can—and most often does—stand independent of proactive religion. True religion does not require the pretense of artistry. "To visit the fatherless and widows in their affliction, and to keep [oneself] unspotted from the world" (James 1:27) needs no "form of comeliness," no rhythm, no rime, and no carefully spun melody. However, art and the divine sit profoundly together, and the combination hopefully will claim a justified place in latter-day Zion.

Taken in Adultery owes its existence to the narrative recorded in the eighth chapter of John. It implicitly refers to the evilness and insensitivity of the accusers and the possibility of forgiveness for the accused. The story explicitly illustrates the perfect understanding of our Savior and confirms his magnanimous persuasion. ❧

ABOUT THE ARTIST

*B*ruce Hixson Smith was born in Salt Lake City, Utah, in 1936. He has been a faculty member in the Art Department at Brigham Young University for more than twenty years. He received his formal education in Utah and New York City.

Two major goals have driven his career as an artist: "One, to acquire the mastery of materials and techniques possessed by the pre-impressionist painters, and two, to place this mastery into the context of a late twentieth century image that would be germane to our society needs," Bruce says. He continues, "My goal has been to place the old master techniques into the context of a late twentieth century image, amalgamating pre-impressionist and modern techniques into an image suitable to our needs at the end of this century."

He has repeatedly combed the literature pertaining to old practices and materials. On a firsthand basis he has carefully studied the images and attitudes of old and modern masters in the major museums of America and Europe. His own canvases have provided a laboratory and testing surface to discover the illusive qualities of the old and modern masters. He has formulated countless painting grounds, mediums, and vehicles, and has even adopted the old practice of grinding all his paint by hand. ❧

Taken in Adultery,
by Bruce Hixson Smith,
36" x 49-1/2", oil, 1995

THE MARTYRDOM

*T*he final act of violence in the life of Joseph Smith occurred when he sealed his testimony with his blood. This situation served as a subject for me to show a relationship between the physical and spiritual sides of the martyrdom. The angels witness the act as if recording it in heaven. The style is expressionistic and symbolic with the use of strong form and exaggerated color. ❧

The Martyrdom, by Gary Smith, 48" x 48", oil on canvas, 1968

ABOUT THE ARTIST

Gary Ernest Smith was born and raised in a relatively isolated farm community 25 miles northeast of Baker, Oregon. Smith's intensity for painting began at a very early age and has progressed through college degrees, numerous commissions and awards, to full-time pursuit of a painting career. The early experiences of his life have taken visual form some 25 years after leaving that demanding rural lifestyle.

Gary's search in art has always been for simplicity and the essence of his subject matter. He does not paint specific events as much as he paints the ambiance of the event. Multiple but related activities may be clustered within a picture or are alluded to, imbuing his subject with symbolism that takes a universal nature. With emphasis on form, symbol, and color, he paints with a passion inspired by first-hand experience. ❧

PORTRAIT OF JOSEPH SMITH

Sutcliffe Maudsley was one of perhaps three artists that allegedly drew or painted Joseph Smith from life. I used his art as a source but reduced my image to a more formal and interpretive style. ❧

TRIUMPHAL ENTRY

*I*n 1982 my wife and I went on a Church painting assignment to the Holy Land. I wanted to experience firsthand the land of the Bible. I enjoyed the challenge of weaving visual design and complex composition into historically significant events in the life of Jesus Christ. ॐ

Triumphal Entry,
by Gary Smith,
48" x 48",
oil on canvas,
1983

THE LAST SUPPER

T wanted to reduce the subject to its essence and get to the significance of the Last Supper. I chose a very straightforward composition with strong form and strong, yet subtle, colors. ∾

The Last Supper, by Gary Smith,
36" x 48", oil on canvas, 1984

Facsimile—Pearl of Great Price, Abraham with Isaac on the Altar

*I*nspired by the Egyptian image in the Pearl of Great Price, I painted a personal interpretation of this significant subject, using imaginative design and color. ∾

Facsimile—Pearl of Great Price, Abraham with Isaac on the Altar, by Gary Smith, 28" x 28", oil on canvas, 1975

CHRIST APPEARING TO THE ELEVEN APOSTLES

I was granted the opportunity to do this painting for my friends at Bonneville Communications. It was used in a video introduction to general conference in the spring of 1987. Presently this painting hangs in the Carthage Illinois Visitors Center. ❧

Christ Appearing to the Eleven Apostles, by Scott McGregor Snow, 48" x 30", oil on canvas, 1987

GOLGOTHA

*P*astels allowed for the very fast creation of this piece. The dark shadows of the hill contrast with the powerful and turbulent sky and the suggestion of three crosses at the top of the hill. Many crucifix paintings have been created; in this one, I felt the need to stand at a distance and feel the power of the earth's mourning. ∾

Golgotha, by Scott McGregor Snow,
20" x 30", pastels on paper, 1986

Old Testament Prophets,
by Scott McGregor Snow,
40" x 30", oil on canvas, 1989

OLD TESTAMENT PROPHETS

$\mathcal{T}$his painting is a realistic depiction of the study of ancient records on parchment by Old Testament prophets. ❧

Nephi Slaying Laban, by Scott McGregor Snow,
36" x 48", oil on canvas, 1992

NEPHI SLAYING LABAN

$\mathcal{F}$or a long time I had visualized this painting. My purpose is to focus on Nephi's dilemma and his ultimate obedience to the Lord. "It is better that one man should perish than that a nation should dwindle and perish in unbelief" (1 Nephi 4:13). ❧

WINTER QUARTERS

*M*y heritage is steeped in Church history. These marvelous ancestors built Nauvoo, served early missions to Europe, marched in Zion's Camp, and walked the distance west to Salt Lake. This painting represents the struggles and sacrifices they made and the amazing organization efforts of the immigration movement and Winter Quarters. This painting hangs in the Winter Quarters Visitors Center. ❧

Winter Quarters,
by Scott McGregor Snow,
60" x 48", oil on canvas, 1994

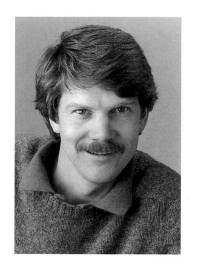

ABOUT THE ARTIST

Scott McGregor Snow was born in Salt Lake City, Utah, and educated early in art by Dale Gibbs and famed local art teacher, Harold Petersen, of Highland High School. Scott later attended Utah State University, graduating in 1978 with a degree in advertising art and design.

He began his professional career with the design firm Level II. In 1980 he left to pursue a freelance career as an illustrator and graphic designer. During these early years he worked for many magazines and book publishers, as well as advertising agencies and companies including the LDS Church, KSL-TV News, CBS, and NBC, where he won numerous national broadcasting awards for his courtroom art. In 1985 he formed a partnership with Randall Royter, establishing Royter Snow Design, an illustration and design firm now in its fourteenth year.

Scott is a member of the New York Society of Illustrators and has been published in many of its annuals. He is chairman of the Salt Lake Community College Advisory Council of the Visual Art and Design Department, and has been an instructor of illustration at the University of Utah. He has won various local and national illustration and design awards.

He is married to Rachelle McDermott of Salt Lake City and is the father of three lovely children who all show artistic promise of their own. ❧

Liz Lemon Swindle

My Servant Joseph

I am not sure when my testimony of the Prophet Joseph Smith turned from a single moment of curiosity to a multitude of powerful witnesses. All the same, I know that Joseph Smith is indeed the Lord's Prophet called to restore this gospel to the earth. Through his sufferings and the sufferings of his family, we each benefit eternally. I am grateful to the Prophet and grateful to the Lord who made this great mission and work a reality. ❧

My Servant Joseph, by Liz Lemon Swindle, 36" x 60", oil on canvas, 1997

About the Artist

*L*iz Lemon Swindle was educated in Utah at Weber State College and Utah State University. Her artwork, shown in galleries throughout the country, reveals exquisite attention to detail. Liz is the recipient of numerous awards, including the Visitors' Choice Award, which she has received twice in international LDS Church competitions. Liz spent many years painting wildlife before focusing her attention on religious topics.

"My spiritual beliefs and roots are planted very deeply, and this allows me to express those feelings to others," Liz says. "I enjoy my art now more than ever before." Her current one-woman show, "Joseph Smith—Impressions of a Prophet," has traveled to many cities nationwide. The show is based on the life of Joseph Smith and deals not only with the events of his life that are most familiar, but especially with the character, emotions, and feelings of Joseph and his family and friends. A book written by Susan Easton Black accompanies the paintings and details the life of Joseph Smith. Liz and her husband, Jon, live in Utah and have five children. ❧

Restoration, by Liz Lemon Swindle, 14" x 11", oil on canvas, 1995

RESTORATION

*W*hat a glorious event to once again have the authority to act in the name of the Lord upon the earth! The darkness had been lifted, and through Joseph Smith the building of the kingdom of God would go forth. I look upon his face and wonder what he felt at just that moment. ❧

EMMA'S HYMNS

*E*mma was very gifted musically. The wife of the Prophet was the obvious choice to be directed of the Lord to compile the hymns for the early Saints. With all the seeming advantages, she still had to organize, delegate, and most of all, rely on her Heavenly Father in order to complete this arduous and overwhelming task; she could not do it alone. ❧

Emma's Hymns,
by Liz Lemon Swindle,
20" x 24", oil, 1997

WHILE EMMA SLEEPS

*J*oseph Smith loved his little family so much and treated that responsibility with the same respect he held for his calling as a prophet of God. His time was often not his own, but I believe he made every attempt to share equally with Emma the tasks of rearing children and caring for a home. ❧

While Emma Sleeps, by Liz Lemon Swindle, 20" x 23", oil on board, 1995

TINY HANDS

*T*he loss of a child is one event in mortality that can only be understood by those parents who have walked the path. The loss of six children is beyond anything I can comprehend in my life experience, and yet Joseph and Emma knew that pain. It would take far less adversity to buckle most of us, but they kept going, ever faithful to the end. ◠

Tiny Hands,
by Liz Lemon Swindle,
20" x 24", oil on canvas, 1996

God Bless You, Mother,
by Liz Lemon Swindle,
9" x 12", oil, 1997

GOD BLESS YOU, MOTHER

I am the mother of the prophet," Lucy declared as she pleaded for assistance to reach her captive sons through an angry mob. Such courage and strength are rare. Is it any wonder that her children would forge through life with anything less? ∾

Heroes, Like Brother Joseph, by Liz Lemon Swindle, 20" x 28", oil, 1996

OF ONE HEART:
JOSEPH AT LIBERTY and EMMA CROSSING THE ICE

*T*he persecutions of Missouri left no member untouched. It was a time when one's beliefs and convictions had to stand on their own strength and merit. No one escaped the refiner's fire. Some were consumed; some emerged triumphant. Joseph and Emma were among the latter. Although their trials were individual, their belief in the Restoration kept them united—"of one heart." They knew the gripping pain of the test and the joy of victory and the overwhelming love of Heavenly Father watching over them. ∽

HEROES, LIKE BROTHER JOSEPH

*T*he world has given us endless heroes to choose from. At first glance there is much to honor and admire. However, a closer look reveals a dearth of values and principles. Fortunately, in Joseph Smith we find a hero worthy of patterning our lives after, not only for the young, but for anyone willing to follow. ∽

Joseph at Liberty, by Liz Lemon Swindle, 36" x 48", oil, 1998
Emma Crossing the Ice, by Liz Lemon Swindle, 26" x 48", 1998

William Whitaker

PIONEER GIRL

I am proud of my pioneer ancestors and I enjoy early Church history. I happen to have a dress from the 1840s in my costume collection. I purchased an old department store dummy from Deseret Industries, put the dress on it, and put a basket of flowers in the hands. The background was a still life prop in the BYU Art Department studios. I had a model whose face and hair looked right for the time, and I painted her from life. ✎

Pioneer Girl, by William Whitaker,
36" x 54", oil on canvas, 1981

HOLLYHOCKS

I have a hard time with too much detail. Certain flowers I find visually comprehensible, others I do not. Hollyhocks are a favorite. During the summer months I locate wonderful beds of hollyhocks all over Provo and Orem. I assume that they have long been an integral part of our Utah culture, since early Utah artists painted them and because they are planted in abundance at This Is the Place State Park. ✍

Hollyhocks, by William Whitaker,
24" x 18", oil on panel, 1997

Steamer Trunk

$\mathcal{I}$ like to put an element of eternity into each of my figure paintings. The seventeenth century painter Vermeer inspired some of the colors in this work. I also happen to have a large collection of antique dresses, many of them purchased in England. ∾

Steamer Trunk, by William Whitaker,
30" x 30", oil on canvas, 1980

About the Artist

$\mathcal{W}$illiam Whitaker was born in Chicago, Illinois, the fourth and only son of W. Ferrin and Martha Basset Whitaker. His father was a fourth-generation Utahn who had moved east and established a successful commercial art studio. William, who by the age of five had already shown natural artistic ability, would often visit his father's firm.

William served an LDS mission to Germany, where he worked as an assistant to the president of the European Mission, Ezra Taft Benson. Upon his return he studied business at the University of Utah and worked for the Evans Advertising Agency in Salt Lake City on LDS Church display projects. Bill did the cover illustration for the first edition of the *Ensign*.

In December of 1967, he graduated from the university with a business degree and worked in Los Angeles at Capital Records as the advertising director. In 1969, he was asked to organize a graphic design program at Brigham Young University. He did so and eventually moved his focus to the fine arts and became an associate professor. In 1985, William and his family moved to Mesa, Arizona, where he lived and painted until 1990. He eventually returned to Provo, Utah, where he still resides, painting six days each week in his studio.

William has painted the portraits of President Howard W. Hunter, President Gordon B. Hinckley, Elder Robert D. Hales, and Elder Henry B. Eyring, among others. ∾

Michael Workman

PIONEER HOME

*T*he small town I live in is said to be the best remaining example of a Mormon village. Spring City, Utah, is full of wonderful pioneer architecture that makes good subject matter for painting—not only for the rich visual textures of the homes themselves, but also for the reminder they are of my Utah heritage. I am especially inspired by the relationship of the architecture with the surrounding landscape as a reminder of the people who lived and worked here. The small stone home in this painting is right outside the door of my studio. ～

ABOUT THE ARTIST

*M*ichael Workman was born in 1959 and raised on a small farm in Highland, Utah, where he learned to love the outdoors and the rural scenes so often depicted in his artwork. He joined the Church in his youth after being taught by a neighbor. Michael served a mission to Melbourne, Australia.

Upon returning from his mission, Michael attended Brigham Young University, majoring in painting and drawing. He worked his way through college as an architectural illustrator, which he continued to do upon graduating. He later returned to BYU to receive a master of fine arts degree.

Michael's work is sold through Meyer Galleries in Santa Fe, New Mexico, and Scottsdale, Arizona. He enjoys teaching workshops in Utah, Texas, and Arizona.

Michael has been featured in several publications, including Don Hagerty's book *Leading the West—100 Contemporary Painters and Sculptors* and Vern Swanson's book *Utah Painting and Sculpture*. He has been featured in *Southwest Art*, *Art Talk*, *Art of the West*, and *Utah Business* magazines.

Michael resides with his wife, Laurel, and their five children—three daughters and two sons—in the small rural town of Spring City, Utah. There he is grateful to be surrounded by beautiful scenery, doing a work that he loves, and dabbling with his own small "gentleman's farm." ～

Pioneer Home, by Michael Workman,
19-1/4" x 12", oil, 1998

*metamorphosis, by Christopher W. Young,
24" x 48", oil on board, 1995*

130

METAMORPHOSIS

I hesitate to explain my work because it seems that the viewer's own interpretation is often more profound than my original meaning. Nevertheless, I offer a few thoughts concerning my painting, *metamorphosis*. The title refers to the transformation that occurs in the life of a butterfly. The three stages, represented by the caterpillar, chrysalis, and the mature butterfly, are beautiful symbols of life, death, and resurrection. I nourish hope in a resurrection because of Jesus Christ, whose coming was announced to Mary by the angel Gabriel. The postcard in the still life represents a fragment from the incredible Ghent altarpiece painted by Jan Van Eyck. The shell, nest, and box represent the physical and mental "cloaks" we try on and replace throughout our earthly journey. I view life as a continual metamorphosis that ultimately can be made beautiful through the atonement of Jesus Christ. ❧

ABOUT THE ARTIST

*C*hristopher Young was born January 30, 1963, in Provo, Utah. Motivated by his father, he developed a love for drawing at an early age. At age nineteen he interrupted his engineering studies at Brigham Young University to serve a mission to Tokyo, Japan. While living there he was highly influenced by Zen art and design. Soon after returning to Utah, he decided to change his major to one in the field of fine art. He again had the opportunity to leave his home, this time to tour Europe's great art museums. While abroad, he became enamored with the early Spanish and Dutch still life painters. Today, Christopher works in his Orem, Utah, studio where he enjoys the support of his wife, Karen, and their four active children.

Christopher's highly detailed, well-crafted paintings create a calm, meditative feeling based on order and simplicity. A trip to his studio might unveil bird's nests, exotic shells, dried flowers, or other natural objects that he arranges for drawings, watercolors, and oil paintings. He says the following concerning his work: "I am captivated by nature's grand design. As we take time to carefully look at seemingly ordinary natural objects, an incredible beauty and harmony is revealed."

Christopher's paintings and prints can be seen at CODA galleries in Park City, Utah, and Palm Desert, California. ❧

Page 15—Lee Udall Bennion artist photo by Jens Lund, courtesy of Utah Arts Council.

Page 30—"Prayer & Dedication of the Salt Lake Valley—Orson Pratt," by VaLoy Eaton, Zions Bank Collection

Page 31—"Jacob Hamblin—Three Strays," by VaLoy Eaton, Zions Bank Collection

Page 33—"First Plowing," by VaLoy Eaton, Zions Bank Collection

Page 54—Brian T. Kershisnik artist photo by John Synder.

Page 56—"Ascent," by David Linn, © The Church of Jesus Christ of Latter-day Saints. Used by permission.

Page 57—"The Conversion of Alma the Younger and the Sons of Mosiah," by David Linn, © The Church of Jesus Christ of Latter-day Saints. Used by permission.

Pages 64-65—"The Eternal Family through Christ," by Judith Mehr, © The Church of Jesus Christ of Latter-day Saints, Museum of Church History and Art. Used by permission.

Page 66—"Moses and the Brazen Serpent," by Judith Mehr, © The Church of Jesus Christ of Latter-day Saints. Used by permission.

Page 79—"Genesis of Repentance," by Wilson Ong, © The Church of Jesus Christ of Latter-day Saints. Used by permission.

Page 80—"Elder Neal A. Maxwell," by Wilson Ong, © The Church of Jesus Christ of Latter-day Saints. Used by permission.

Page 83—"The First Vision," by Del Parson, © The Church of Jesus Christ of Latter-day Saints. Used by permission.

Page 85—"The Greatest of All (Christ in Gethsemane)," by Del Parson, © The Church of Jesus Christ of Latter-day Saints. Used by permission.

Page 106—"The Martyrdom," by Gary Smith, © The Church of Jesus Christ of Latter-day Saints. Used by permission.

Page 108—"Triumphal Entry," by Gary Smith, courtesy of Blaine T. Hudson

Page 109—"The Last Supper," by Gary Smith, courtesy of Donald Boulter

Page 111—"Christ Appearing to the Eleven Apostles," by Scott MacGregor Snow, © The Church of Jesus Christ of Latter-day Saints. Used by permission.

Page 112—"Golgotha," by Scott MacGregor Snow, © The Church of Jesus Christ of Latter-day Saints. Used by permission.

Page 113—"Old Testament Prophets," by Scott MacGregor Snow, © The Church of Jesus Christ of Latter-day Saints. Used by permission.

Pages 114-15—"Winter Quarters," by Scott MacGregor Snow, © The Church of Jesus Christ of Latter-day Saints. Used by permission.